The STRUGGLE WITHIN

Daniel Burks

ISBN 978-1-0980-4302-5 (paperback)
ISBN 978-1-0980-4303-2 (digital)

Copyright © 2020 by Daniel Burks

All rights reserved. No part of this publication may be reproduced, distributed, or transmitted in any form or by any means, including photocopying, recording, or other electronic or mechanical methods without the prior written permission of the publisher. For permission requests, solicit the publisher via the address below.

Christian Faith Publishing, Inc.
832 Park Avenue
Meadville, PA 16335
www.christianfaithpublishing.com

Printed in the United States of America

This book is for all who passed away:

Paul Huntsman
(1949–2014)

Thelma Nanny
(1930–2019)

Edna Susan Burks
(1954–2013)

Douglas Madderra
(1947–2009)

Nellie Louise Burks
(1931–2015)

Leroy Fitzgerald
(1935–1991)

Jesse Burks
(1919–2000)

Donna Burks
(1952–2014)

Contents

Chapter 1: Rough Beginnings 7
Chapter 2: Family 15
Chapter 3: Fear 23
Chapter 4: Grandpa Leroy 31
Chapter 5: The Cult 38
Chapter 6: Evil 46
Chapter 7: New Beginnings 54
Chapter 8: Tragedies 63
Chapter 9: Wedding 71
Chapter 10: Life 79
Chapter 11: Diagnosed 86

1

Rough Beginnings

On the morning of December 27, 1980, my mom Diana had a job at a pipe factory in Washington, Missouri. While making smoking pipes one day, a tall guy was pushing a dolly with soda on it. He was working for a Coca-Cola company in Washington. He wasn't there long, just filling up the soda machines briefly, yet it was an encounter that would prove significant.

Meanwhile, Diana was going on a small vacation. At that time, she was still living at home with her mom and some of her brothers and sisters. Others moved out and started families of their own. As 1981 approached, my mom stayed friendly, kindhearted, and willing to help anyone she thought might have needed it. She was a good Christian woman, having been raised in the church. My family grew up in the United Pentecostal church in Washington, Missouri. They worked for what they got and stayed content with the life God give them. After moving out of her parents' house Mom struggle living from paycheck to paycheck, but as the summer ended, it marked her second year with the company.

The guy returned with the dolly. After getting acquainted on one of Diana's lunch breaks, it was clear that both wanted to date. Apparently, they went back up to Jason's house for a one-night stand. Diana and Jason weren't using protection at that time. Diana probably thought she wasn't going to get pregnant. However, due to both hormones and perhaps sudden choices, Jason took whatever led to that moment. It became clear that Diana and Jason were moving quickly. Many would say nothing is worse than marriage from unplanned pregnancy. Diana thought she might of have gotten the flu from work because she was puking in the morning. Diana's doctor told her well it was not the flu. Her doctor or her mom thought she might be pregnant. Diana went to get a pregnancy test, which came back positive.

Diana saw Jason putting sodas in the machine. She went up to him and said, "I am pregnant with your baby." He just stood there looking at Diana for a while before saying, "That's not my baby."

Diana ran to her mom's house, crying all the way home after work. She was heartbroken, feeling lonely but helpless. Thankfully, her mom encouraged her. My grandma was very old-fashioned. She didn't believe in having sex till she's married. She always went by what the Bible said, but Diana was already out of high school and working on getting an apartment. By the end of 1981, Diana found out that she was pregnant with a little baby boy. The doctor told her due date is in September 1982. She didn't know what day yet so as time went by, Diana's stomach got bigger and bigger. Diana was a single woman working at a pipe factory. Her employer put her on maternity leave after a certain time. Diana had to get maternity clothes to wear and had to move out of her own apartment to go stay with her mom in case anything happened to the baby. The pipe factory told her to come back after the baby was born, but Diana told her boss she wanted to keep working while she was carrying me.

Diana still tried to get a hold of Jason to let him about his son, but Jason kept denied that it was his baby. Jason was an alcoholic and had very bad anger issues. I always believed he didn't care about Diana and me or anyone else for that matter, plus he was a smoker. So a few short months before Diana was about to give birth to me, she finally agreed to stop working. Diana was very was hurt by the way Jason got her pregnant. Throughout the years, she wasn't happy about him not calling or coming to check on her while she was pregnant. Jason never paid child support in his life. Diana never even saw a cent. Diana or my grandma never had any money to get a lawyer to take Jason to court. When Diana did have money, she used it to buy baby stuff.

THE STRUGGLE WITHIN

In September, Diana could have the baby at any moment. She was starting to get very excited and nervous about the due date. My grandma was more excited than scared or nervous. On September 22, 1982, she tried one more time to convince Jason to him help her with the baby, but still no call or visit. Very late at night, her contractions started. Diana left a message on Jason's phone, telling him that she had to go to the hospital right away since she was in labor. Her mother had to take Diana to a hospital in St. Louis, Missouri at 2:30 a.m. At the hospital, there was still no sign of Jason anywhere when his first child was born at 4:30 a.m. on September the 23, 1982. Soon my grandma and mother were picking out some baby names. My grandma gave me the name Daniel. I wish she picked out a cool, awesome name like Nathaniel, but Diana agreed to call me Daniel. Since Diana and I were doing so great, they told us we could go home the very next day.

Diana knew she would have a long and stressful time raising me all by herself, but her family all helped Diana raise me from time to time. A month went by, we still haven't heard from Jason. Diana was planning to take me to see Jason and show him his newborn baby boy. On October 8, Diana took me to show Jason his baby that Jason and Diana creative. When Diana went to Jason's house, he didn't give crap about me. He told Diana to get the "little bastard" out of his house. He didn't want to see me or Diana ever again. That really hurt Diana. I think that's why she never talk about Jason as I got older. After that, Diana didn't hear from Jason ever again.

A short time later in early 1983, Diana moved back to her apartment. For a few months, Diana went back and forth to her apartment and her mom's house. One day, Diana met a man named Paul, he lives in Union Missouri at the time. He took care of me, and Diana was very happy that she found someone finally to help her raise me. He was the dad that would change my diapers. A few short months later, Paul and Diana went out they would. I was just a baby, about to turn a month old. Sometimes when Paul or Diana went out, they would drop me off at Diana's mom house or Diana would have Paul's mom babysit me. Every Thanksgiving and Christmas, we would either go to Paul's mom's house or my grandma's house. We lived in Union Missouri, so we didn't mind driving back and forth to both grandmas' houses.

At one time before I turned a year old, Paul was in the bedroom and Diana was in the living room when I started walking. Jason was missing out on everything from crawling to walking. Every Sunday, Paul, Diana, and both grandparents would take me in the of the church. I didn't really learn about God till I was two years old. I was trying to say God at seven months old, instead I would say, "Dad." Diana and Paul was pretty shocked when I said dad and not mom. It was April 28, 1983. Diana and Paul got married a year after I was born on May 5. By that time, I was already walking. They had a hard time trying to keep me away from everything. On May 20, we moved to St. Clair Missouri, to a trailer that my uncle bought for Paul and Diana as a wedding gift. That spring, I wanted to go out and play. Summer was coming next month so it was going to get hot outside. Then my uncle came over and put in a new air conditioner so we could stay cool in the summer. We had fans in the house, which also helped a little bit.

When was a kid, I actually didn't know that Paul was not my real dad. No one would talk about it, like a secret I never knew about. I would be confused when Diana talked to Paul about the "last" man. He never mention who this other guy was. I didn't know what kind of work he did. I never even knew about Paul background. All I could say is that Diana and Paul took great care of me when I was very sick and took me to the doctor. The doctor told them I had walking pneumonia. I was sick a lot as a baby. The doctors would give me meds. Four weeks later, I would start to feel a lot better. I could have died if I never got to the doctors. Diana would read the Bible to me every night when I went to bed. It was summertime and I couldn't go outside because I still had pneumonia, though a lot better. I was so ready for my birthday because I wanted to eat grown-up food. By the end of summer, I was getting ready for my first birthday. I was born on the day of autumn. My parents threw me a birthday party. I was the happiest baby, smiling and running around. Paul cleaned up the house after the party while Diana gave me a bath.

October was right around the corner. In the next few weeks, Diana and Paul went shopping at Walmart. I saw these scary masks that freaked me out. I didn't know what they were. I just sat there in that shopping cart and stared at them. There was no bad love in this family. We were all happy. I was still curious about the strange guy. During Halloween, my parents took me trick-or-treating for the first time, but I didn't get to eat the candy. Diana and Paul thought I was too young to have any because I might choke on it.

Later that year, my mom started getting sick again, puking in the morning. Paul took her to the doctors the next day. We all thought she came down with the flu. We were at home watching television when the doctor called Diana and Paul to tell them that they're going to have a baby. We had no idea what the sex was because Diana wasn't ready to know whether it was a boy or girl.

Every night before bed, it would be the same routine. But one day, Diana put on some music as she turned off the lights. Some doo-wop music on the radio would put me to sleep very quickly. Throughout Diana's pregnancy, Diana and Paul would drop me off at grandma's when they went to the amusement park. At grandma's house, I would play with my toys. The amusement park was located between St. Clair Missouri to Eureka Missouri, about a thirty-minute drive. It was pretty late when they got back so they called Diana's mom to keep me overnight. They came to get me the next morning. The next day, it was a warm spring day. They decided we should all go to the zoo. Paul and Diana took turns pushing the baby stroller with me in it. After a while, I was apparently trying to get out because I was tired of sitting inside that hot. Every time I would see an animal, I got very excited about it. It was fun driving down there and back. We would listen to fifties music, the decade Diana was born in. She couldn't do too much since she was six months pregnant. I had such a blast at the zoo. We really didn't visit too much during the summertime because it was too hot, especially for my pregnant mom.

As far as I remember, my life was normal till I found out a dark secret when I was older. I went to my first funeral when I was about a year and a half years old sometime in 1984. It was a very frightening experience. I have never seen a dead body before. Diana was about to give birth to her second child, another little boy. Paul and Diana were getting very excited about having a little baby in the house since I was growing up.

My brother arrived on October 16, 1984. Diana's water broke before she even got to the hospital. They name him Douglas. As I watched Diana and Paul welcome a newborn, there was just so much excitement. Everybody was so happy. I was also happy about having a little brother. Diana and Paul did the best they could to give us both the attention. They even took us to the park in late October. Diana and Paul didn't want us to get sick so we had to wear coats. As a little kid, I would take my coat off, not listening to anyone half of time. As kids often do, we got sick even if we had our coats on, but we got through it. This would be my little brother's first Halloween and my second, but I still didn't get to eat any candy despite crying my butt off. Before my parents let me eat it, they checked the candy to make sure nothing was in it.

The next holiday we would have was Thanksgiving. To prepare, Diana went shopping for food at Walmart. As soon we got back, the phone rang. It was Diana's mother-in-law, Paul's mom. She wanted to come up for Thanksgiving this year. My grandparents always baby us, but Paul and Diana didn't like us getting spoiled too much. We would do this every year. I love my grandparents. I was so happy that God kept this family together. It was such a peaceful and loving family who went to church every Sunday. Little baby Douglas got save at the church on this gathering on November 25, 1984, just a little over a week since Thanksgiving.

On the last day of November, Diana and Paul took me to my grandma's house. Diana's parents was divorced so it was just my grandma and my aunt living there. Diana's twin sister was living with their mom. She was disabled so she never got married or had any kids at all. Since my aunt couldn't have any kids, she just spoiled her two nephews. Diana and Paul were doing their Christmas shopping. When they were all done with shopping, wrapped up the gifts, and hid them in the closet, they came to pick us up. We were already sleeping.

On December 4, my grandpa Leroy, Paul's stepdad, called Diana and Paul about visiting for Christmas. He wanted to see his grandchildren. We were so excited. Not so much my brother since at that time, he was still crawling and didn't know what was going on. Grandpa Leroy arrived ten days before Christmas. He said he would see us every April, right after Easter. He also invited us out for barbecue and brought us a bunch of Christmas gifts. Grandpa Leroy was actually one of my favorite Grandparent's. My parents told him as a joke that he was going to turn us into brats. Grandpa Leroy just laughed. After we opened all of our gifts, Grandpa sat down in the recliner to watch his favorite Western shows, taking off his boots. He would always fall asleep through it. While he was snoozing away, Diana or Paul would try to change the station on the television, but he would tell them to turn it back to his favorite shows. He must have had one eye open. I still can't figure it out how he did. When he woke up, he would put his boots back on, pick us up to hug and kiss us, and told Paul and Diana he would call them in April. As Grandpa Leroy was heading back, the snow started to fall so he got out before the snow fell hard. When Grandpa Leroy got home, he called Diana and let her know that he got home safe.

The next day, it was Christmas. Douglas and I got to open our presents Paul and Diana helped Douglas open his. As for me, I just shredded my wrapping paper. We were so happy. It was also snowing outside so we ended up having a white Christmas. After we got our gifts, Diana and Paul let us go out and play. Diana had to help Douglas because the snow was deep. We enjoyed ourselves, even more when Grandpa Leroy called Diana and Paul to wish us a Merry Christmas. For the rest of that day, we just watched movies. Just in a couple of days later, Diana and Paul were up very late to watch the new year coming in while me and Doug were in bed. The year 1984 was a great year for our family with baby being our biggest moment.

As I was getting bigger, my brother was now walking. What surprise us was that he was starting to talk, saying "mommy" and "daddy." The beginning of 1985 was a cold winter. In the morning, Grandpa Leroy called to see how everyone was doing. Diana picked up the phone and started chatting with Grandpa Leroy, asking him how his Christmas and New Year's went. He told Diana it was great. Everybody was so happy at Christmas and New Year's. We got to play with our new toys in our room. While Diana got off the phone with Grandpa Leroy, Paul started taking down the decorations and the lights. They put the Christmas tree back into the box and the lights into a bag. After everything was taking down, they finally sat down and watch movies. It was too cold to be outside, and my brother was running all over the place. Diana and Paul had to get him before he breaks anything. We are all hanging out in the living with our toys.

The next day, the phone rang. It was Paul's mother, asking how our Christmas went. They told her we loved all the presents that we got from them. We were planning to visit Diana's divorced parents. We went to see Diana's dad first but he was just a disrespectful so we just left. We went to visit Diana's mom the next day. In the next few weeks, we just stayed home since we did too much traveling.

One day, Diana and Paul were drinking coffee at the table and talking about what we were doing this spring and summer. We were supposed to go to Grandpa Leroy's house for barbecue but then Paul called his mom to see she wanted to come up and have a barbecue with all of us. She said yes. Our family loved to be together and enjoyed each other's company. Diana's mom called and ended up getting invited to the barbecue on the following weekend as well. At that time, Diana's mom and sister live out in the country. So we all were planning to go out for an adventure since Paul's mom was coming up. The next day, Paul's mom came and spent two weeks with us. Our first adventure was at the science center. That's the first time we had been there. We thought it was going to be very boring, but actually it really wasn't. We saw whole bunch of cool dinosaurs.

Since it was a warm breezy day, we decided to head to the zoo. We spent about four hours there. After we left the zoo, we all had a picnic at the park. It was a blast. At home, Doug and I were in the living room while Diana, Paul, and his mom were drinking coffee in the kitchen. They didn't care what time it was.

2

Family

On the afternoon of April 16, 1985, Douglas and were playing outside on a bright sunny day. We had some new neighbors moving right next door to us. They came up to us to introduce themselves. After they shook hands, Diana and Paul welcomed the new residents to the neighborhood. They had three daughters and seem like very nice people. The Smith kids always came over and play with us if they saw us outside. We got to know each other as time went on. They were the greatest neighbors. My brother was walking and talking a little more.

Their middle daughter, Stephanie Smith, came over to see if me and my brother can come out and play. Diana would watch my brother join in the kickball game. If it was very warm, a small pool would be set up for all of us to swim in, though we would have to take turn to get in and out of it the pool because it was not big enough for all of us to get in there. There was a lot of neighborhood kids out and about on a Saturday afternoon. We never had to walk that far to go swimming because there was a pool at the top of the hill we could go to. My parents would always be outside with us to make sure that we weren't going to be kidnapped. Diana and Paul were always cautions about us being outside by ourselves. They wouldn't let us do till we got older. Douglas and I had great parents who kept us out of trouble. People always told them, "You have two sweet and kind little boys." That made us and my parents feel special. Diana and Paul always cared and protected us. I was turning three years old this, and Douglas was turning a year old. My parents told us to be on our best behavior when we go somewhere.

One day, we were watching some sporting event ion TV in late August. Diana and Paul loved major league baseball. If it was a rainy day, we would watch baseball or maybe some preseason football. We always begged to let us play outside in the rain so we could wear our swimming trunks on and splash around in big puddles. It was just us being kids. I asked I asked my parents if I could play baseball when I get older. My parents' answered, "If we have the money, you can."

Jason wasn't around to see me growing up. I was pretty sure he was home drinking and didn't even care about me. I still had no clue why he wasn't around. I kept having fun as kid and hanging out with my friends. Around September, I was turning four in a couple of weeks. Grandpa Leroy called to let Diana and Paul know that he was inviting us to come over for another barbecue. We were so excited about seeing him again. It was a cold rainy day when we all went out there for dinner. Diana kept us inside because she didn't want us to run outside without our jackets. Diana and Paul told us that if we put our jackets on, we could come outside. We did so later on that night. After we got home, we watched a scary movie. I was three. My brother was already in bed, but I wanted to stay up and watch television that night. I heard my parents talking about the movie *Silver Bullet*, which was based on novel by Stephen King. The movie was about a Baptists minster who actually turn into a werewolf. I would be four in the next week. I couldn't wait to watch more horror movies. Horror movies never affected me in anyway. The next night, I watched John Carpenter's *Halloween*. It was a great movie! I love it. I didn't have nightmares from those movies at all. A week later, I turned four years old. Now that I was getting older, I could watch any hardcore horror movie as long as it was my birthday. I got to watch *Halloween* again.

Douglas' birthday was coming up just as the leaves were changing colors and falling from the trees. I love the fall. It's one of my favorite times of the year. Mom and Dad would rake the leaves up for us then we would jump in the pile. Football season was already in progress. We love watching it. Toward the end of September, it was a cold rainy day outside so we all decided to stay in. Diana cooked chili that night. It was a Sunday, and we would watch either movies or football. Diana and Paul would take us outside once in a while if it wasn't raining. We all would gather our friends to play football. My brother couldn't play because he was barely two years old. We didn't play tackle, just two-hand touch football. Douglas would stay in with Diana while she cooked. Paul was outside, watching me play. On October 3, a Saturday, we went down to the flea market. Every weekend, except maybe Sundays, we would go to church with my grandma and aunt. After church, we went to the caverns give us something to do on a Sunday afternoon. We would stay till closing time. Then we would all go home. Diana would cook supper. After we were done eating, Diana would give us a bath while Paul would be doing the dishes. After our baths, Douglas and I would brush our teeth and would stay up for a little until Diana said, "Bedtime, boys."

On October 10 on a Friday afternoon, I was playing with my toys in my room and Douglas was in his room. Diana and Paul yelled, "Boys, come into the kitchen quick. We have a question to ask you." They asked if we would like to go out to dinner and go see a movie or have dinner and go to Walmart. They didn't they didn't have much to give but they gave us a little spending money. Diana was still working at the pipe factory at that time. We ended up going to our favorite pizza shack. We would always get the supreme pizza, our family's favorite. If we had leftovers food, we would eat it for the next day. Then we went to Walmart where bought my first Halloween decoration ever. I thought it was a cool decoration to hang up in my bedroom. In just a few days, my little brother would be two years old.

On Sunday, October 15, we went to church for Sunday services. After church, our whole family would go out to eat. My grandma would pay for dinner. It wasn't too expensive since it was a cheap restaurant that they had great food. After that, we decide to head back home and called it a day. On October 16, it was my brother's second birthday. My brother Douglas had a great birthday. Diana and Paul made sure the bills were paid, there was food on the table, and we always had clothes to wear. The next day, we all went to the pumpkin patch. Our parents never told us where we were going or anything. They said it was a surprise. If Mom and Dad had extra money, they would spend it on us. Diana was working. Paul was getting a check as a disabled veteran. On October 27, we all gathered outside to play in the leaves Diana and Paul raked up. My brother and I would jump into a big pile of leaves. After a while, we decide to run to the store to get pumpkin bags to put the leaves in. Douglas and would play around with the leaves right before Diana and Paul put them in the bag.

My grandparents were Pentecostal. If they knew we were watching horror movies, they would yell at Diana and Paul because they didn't care for those kinds of movies at all. However, Diana and Paul always told us that the movies were faked by Hollywood. On October 29, we had to run to Walmart to get our costumes. Thank God that Diana and Paul had the money that year for Halloween. Douglas went as Jason, and I was a cowboy. We also bought a jack-o'-lantern. When we got home, Diana and Paul carved the pumpkin on the table as we watched. Once they were done, they put a candle inside it and lit it up. We then put it on the porch outside. Douglas and I were all too happy to keep opening the door to check on it. The only problem was when it was going to be cold and rainy. We had to keep warm for our parents to take us out trick-or-treating.

Diana was making pretty good money at the pipe factory so we went out for dinner at McDonalds once we were done trick-or-treating. On October 31, we were so excited about trick-or-treating. Earlier that day, we took a nap to make sure we had a enough energy to make it through the night. It was raining all day on Halloween. The year 1985 was a great year. We had a lot of family gatherings. It was a fun evening. After we got back home from McDonald's, Mom and Dad passed out a lot of our candy because we couldn't eat all of it and my brother was too young to eat it anyway. We turned the porch light on and waited for the trick-or-treaters to come. Later, we watched some horror movie till it was time to brush our teeth and get ready for bed.

The next holiday was Thanksgiving then Christmas and New Year's. Diana always had a scripture in the Bible to read to us that would make us feel safe while we slept at night along with some music. It was a Saturday morning on November 1 that we got a phone call from Diana's mom. She told Paul and Diana that she could take us, the kids, to give them a break. They dropped us off at grandma's house. That night, Aunt and Grandma tucked us in bed and also read us a Bible verse. We love that our parents and relatives read the Bible to us. The next morning, they took us out for breakfast. By the time we got back at 10:30 a.m., Diana and Paul were waiting for us and Douglas went over to hug our parents.

On the morning of the November 2, it was starting to snow in Indiana. It was cold, and the wind was blowing. You can see the trees and power lines swaying back and forth. That night, Diana made chili for our family. She invited her mom and twin sister over for dinner, but they planned to stay home and stay warm since it was snowing hard. Mom and Dad just watched TV. Since it was a Saturday, we got to sleep on the floor in the living room.

The next day, we all went to church and then we went grocery shopping. My parents got paid on the first so we had to get stuff for Thanksgiving. Sometimes Paul would go to the veteran's hospital for a checkup. That Tuesday, we all went down to the VA hospital. As a four-year-old, I ended up pulling the fire alarm. I didn't know what it was or what it was for. Everyone came running. Diana came over and asked, "Did you or your brother pull that?" I said that I did it and started laughing about it I thought it was funny. One man who worked in the building shut off the alarm. Then he came over to my family, shaking his finger at me and saying, "Santa is not going to bring you anything good for Christmas if you don't behave yourself. He's always watching." After we left, Diana and Paul gave me a heart-to-heart talk not pulling the emergency alarm again. I was just a kid, but I did learn my lesson.

Then we all went to Kmart. We saw a lot of Christmas decorations. Diana and Paul bought a Christmas tree. We saw the big guy himself. I was afraid of Santa Claus. I thought he would hurt me or my brother, but he didn't. Diana made me embarrassed when she told Santa that I pulled the fire alarm. They both look at me disapprovingly. Then she told Santa that I was very curious. After a while, we all joked about it, even Santa laughed. Then he repeated what Diana told me that it was only for emergency. He also told me that he's been watching me. He said, "You have been a good little boy this year." Douglas also sat on his lap. Santa asked him what he wanted for Christmas. At that time, we still believed in Santa when he said, "I see what I can do this year."

On the night of November 16, Diana came into my room while I was trying to pray. I asked God for forgiveness. Paul was in the kitchen watching television when Diana burst in to tell Paul I was praying on my own. She was so happy for me. The next day, Diana and Paul decided to take us to her mom's house so she could go Thanksgiving shopping. As kids, we were always begging for new toys or our favorite snacks. Douglas and I weren't angels at all. Diana and Paul were firm when they told us we needed to save our money for groceries or bills when we would throw a big fit.

Then on the morning of November 24, just a couple of days before Thanksgiving, Diana would thaw the turkey and prepare everything out to put on the stove for the big feast. Well, on that same day, Grandpa Leroy called Diana to ask if he could come for Thanksgiving, and sure enough, he did. I was so excited to see my favorite grandpa. On the big day, Douglas and I were sitting on the floor, watching the Macy's Thanksgiving Day Parade and Santa Claus coming into town. After the parade was over, we turned then channel over to watch the football game. Grandpa Leroy didn't arrive to the house till later. It was bitter cold outside. I didn't want to go out and get sick. We always tried to outsmart our parents by sneaking outside to play, but they were right. At about 4:00 p.m., Grandpa Leroy came over and brought food so there was a lot of leftovers. While everybody was sitting in the chair in the kitchen, Douglas was sitting in a highchair and making a mess with his dinner. Grandpa Leroy was talking about Christmas shopping. He said, "I know what I can get for the boys this year." We were so excited for Christmas. We couldn't wait what we were going to get.

After Thanksgiving, my parents started putting up the Christmas tree. We had fun watching Diana and Paul put lights and ornaments on it. Diana put the angel on top. When they turned on the tree, it was very bright and shiny. Since Christmas and New Year's was coming up, Mom and Dad were planning to do shopping on a Saturday when her sister and mom could watch us. It was the very last day of November, my parents would be getting paid so they could pay bills, buy food, and go Christmas shopping for us kids. Diana called her mom and sister to ask them if we could spend the night with them and go to church in the morning. Because Diana and Paul had more shopping to do, we spent time at grandma's house. On Sunday, December 2, we all waited for Mom and Dad to pick us up. They finally came for us at around 5:00 p.m. Then we went home. After dinner, we washed our hands, wiped our mouths, and watched Christmas movies on television.

One night, we all were watching the news on the television, and there was prediction for a white Christmas. On the 15th, just a couple of weeks away from Christmas, Grandpa Leroy called Paul and Diana. Grandpa Leroy loved Diana. They were very close. Paul's stepdad told them that he will come over a couple of days before Christmas. He said, "Instead of cooking this year, how about I bring some pizzas?" Diana said, "That's fine. You're giving me a break from cooking." Grandpa Leroy decided to visit on Saturday. He brought dinner and our presents. We were so grateful for him On December 22 at noon, he called Diana and told her, "I had to stop by the store really quick to pick up a few more items." When he got to the house, Diana and Paul and Grandpa Leroy were carrying a lot of stuff into the house. It was cloudy and looked like it was going to snow. Grandpa Leroy asked Diana and Paul, "What would you like to do first, open Christmas gifts or have pizza?" Mom and Dad choose to open the gifts first. Grandpa Leroy got me Ghostbusters Play-doh set. It was so slimy but very fun to play with. He also got Douglas some Play-Doh. We ended up getting it in our hair so Diana had to give us a bath. Grandpa Leroy got Diana some new pots and pans. He gave Paul some new tools and a tool bag. Grandpa Leroy stayed over till bout seven o'clock at night. We didn't even know but it was snowing outside, it was coming down so hard. We had to wake grandpa up. Grandpa Leroy put on his boots and got his keys off the table. He had to get home before the weather got too bad.

After Grandpa left, we all decided to look at Christmas lights so we jumped into the car and headed out in the snow. Diana turned on the car radio. One of my favorite songs came on, Elvis Presley's song, "If Every Day Was Like Christmas." I love that song, it reminds of Grandpa Leroy. It's been my favorite Christmas tune, even today I still listen to that song.

3

Fear

By 1988, I was six years old, soon to be seven, and my brother was going to be five. On March 8, 1988, Diana was having trouble with her right arm. Paul said, "Maybe it's just you working too much. You need to rest your right arm. If it gets worse, then we can take you to the doctors." Paul decided to take Diana to the doctors. They took X-rays. Well, it wasn't her arm, it was her neck. Paul had to take her to a specialist at the hospital. They told her she was going to need surgery. Right around early spring, Diana had to inform the pipe factory that she had to have neck surgery. So the specialist told her to bring her back one more time on April 15 to schedule the surgery. They went ahead and set it up for July 22, 1988. She was so scared and nervous that she didn't want to do it. She knew she would be in pain for the rest of her life so she had no choice.

We decided to go out and have fun because after surgery, Diana wouldn't be able to do anything for quite a while. Since it was so nice outside, we decided to head to the zoo and the science center, maybe to the mall. It all depends what time we were done at the zoo and the science center. It was only 2:00 p.m. so we headed to the zoo. The first place we saw was the gorillas. Diana had to sit down because her legs were very tried. She had to lean against the window. The gorilla came from behind and hit the window hard, which scared Diana to death. Then the gorilla turned around and just stared at Diana. She told Paul to take her somewhere else. We all laughed. Next we sat down at the zoo restaurant. By 5:00 p.m., we just went home and had dinner.

Summer was around the corner. As her surgery date was coming up, Diana was in a panic. Paul had to calm her down. This was a major surgery. I think everyone is scared when they have surgery done. To distract her, we bought pizza and rented *Halloween, Silver Bullet*, and other movies from the video store. We made sure Diana kept her mind off the surgery. Finally, July 22 came around. All of us had to be up very early to go to the hospital at around six o'clock in the morning. She went in to get prep for surgery while we sat around in the waiting room. They wheeled her for surgery at 8:30 a.m. It lasted for a good eight hours. The doctors kept coming out every four hours. It was very scary to think we would all lose Diana, but we prayed to God to make sure she was in good hands with the doctors. After eight hours, the doctors told us the good news that she did great on the table but we had to wait till she woke up so they could take her up to her room. The nurse came in because Diana was asking for all of us She had to stay in the hospital for a few days so nothing would go wrong. Diana was in a great deal of pain, but she was a trooper and had God on her side. Before we made it home, her mom, twin sister, brother, and sister came to see her. Even Grandpa Leroy and Paul's mom visited her. The doctor told Paul she could go home on Monday but she had to come back for a checkup in a couple months. As the weekend ended, we were all ready for Diana to come home with us. As Monday came around, Diana was so happy to finally come home. She didn't want to be in the hospital anymore.

We didn't get to celebrate my or Douglas' birthday. On October 16, she went back for a follow-up. The doctors told her that a pressed nerve cut circulation in her right arm, paralyzing it. We didn't even go out trick-or-treating or passed out any candy that year. Diana mom's called and invited us to her house for Thanksgiving this year. Instead of cooking anything, we all went to Diana's mom's house. Diana's twin sister and mom cooked for all of us.

On September 21, just two days left till fall, I was about to turn eight years old and Douglas was about to turn six. We were moving up in school. September was a great month. As the summer ended,

THE STRUGGLE WITHIN

I was looking forward to Halloween and couldn't wait till we go out trick-or-treating. We picked out our Halloween costumes for that year. Halloween was one of my favorite holidays, but it wouldn't be much longer. On October 27, 1989, three days from Halloween, Douglas and I were preparing for trick-or-treating. Diana and Paul called us in the kitchen right after school and told us what our plans were for Halloween night. They had surprise for us. We were going out to dinner first then we will come back to put our costumes on. We went to our favorite pizza shack. On October 31, we got home from school and went straight to the pizza place. Once dinner, we went back home to put our costumes on. I was Batman and Douglas was Ghostface. The weather wasn't too bad so went out to some of the houses that had porch lights on. Diana told Paul we will give away candy once we got back to the house. After a little over an hour of trick-or-treating, we went home and turned the porch light on. Diana said, "Paul, could you make us some coffee?" Then we watched some horror movies on television as Paul was making coffee.

A couple of masked figures came up to Diana. We had so much candy. Diana wanted to save some for her and Paul. They didn't like that. Diana saw their Texas license plate as they were parked in our driveway. Both masked figures pulled out two razor blades and sliced Diana's right arm open. We heard her screaming and yelling. When she came in, I saw the blood dripping from a big gash on her arm. Paul called 911. At that moment, I was very mad. The police came. They thought Paul did it. Diana told them he was inside making coffee. Her arm was wrapped up with a towel when the ambulance came. Just a few mins later, the police chief arrived. He was very angry with what happened. One of the neighbors came over as Paul walked with the paramedics to the ambulance. I wanted to go out after those masked figures that changed my family's life forever. I was in shock. I just stood there glaring. I had nowhere to turn to. I was an eight-year-old boy. Douglas and I were so worried four our mom. The neighbor lady stayed with us while Paul had follow the ambulance to the hospital. The thing is, our mom didn't even feel the blade digging into her arms. I couldn't cry, I was so mad. At the hospital, Paul called the neighbor lady they made it to the hospital.

They didn't get back home till three in the morning. Douglas and I were in bed me. In my mind, I wanted to seek revenge on those two. I couldn't sleep. Paul told the neighbor Diana needed fifty stitches. They were at the hospital for five and half hours. Diana and Paul were furious about what happen.

By four in the morning, though we barely got any sleep, we got out of bed. Paul fixed us some breakfast. Diana was awake but was in so much pain, she had to take her meds. Paul made coffee for her and Diana. I went outside with Douglas and Paul. We found two razor blades on the ground. Paul went into the house to call the police back to collect fingerprint samples. When the police came, they brought two baggies to put the blades in.

I asked myself why this was happening to our family. Why would someone attack Diana on Halloween? An eight-year-old is not supposed to see this kind of violence. It only happened on horror movies. I really thought I was dreaming. I suspected that whoever did this might not be done with Diana yet. As I went into my room, I knew this was going to be war I have to find out who did it and get them before they harm anyone else. All the fear turned into hate for me. For hours, I was blaming God for what happened. I wanted to turn my back against him. I wanted vengeance on those two. I never thought I would have a dark mind and think evil thoughts. At eight years old, I didn't know what it means to have such anger or hate for anyone, which is not God fault. What I was planning in my mind was pure evil. I ask my parents why does bad things happen to good people was I confused. I was starting to get cold-hearted. I didn't know what else to do. I kept watching horror movies to make me feel better. Maybe it was a way to hide the pain inside or make excuses. I was really hurting with what happened.

After Halloween, we were all trying to move on with our lives and just be happy. Our neighbors would come check on Diana. Her mom, her twin sister, Paul's mom, and so Grandpa Leroy also called to check on her. When Diana told him what happened, Grandpa Leroy wasn't happy either. As Christmas and Thanksgiving passed by, we weren't going to let any masked figure mess with us. The New Year offered a fresh start. By January 3, 1990, we haven't heard anything from the police if they caught them or if they went back to Texas. All I knew was that they were nowhere to be found around our town. I wasn't going to give up hope at finding them. I don't care how long it will take me to find them. I will hunt them down till I am dead. I couldn't stop thinking about what happened that night. I tried to find something to do to keep my mind off the horrible crime. I was just going to think about Diana and Paul's wedding anniversary. Even though I was upset at God, I still wanted him and his angels to watch over us.

Every night, I could hear Diana screaming. I would cry in my sleep. I didn't tell Diana or Paul about it, just kept it all too myself. As February came around, all I could see was Diana running through the door. It was horrible that someone could do that to her. I thought Halloween was supposed to be fun, not have innocent people get hurt. I had to find every way to put on a happy face for Diana and Paul. I didn't want them to know anything was wrong. I even had to hide it at school. I didn't want anyone asking me if there's anything wrong. I didn't want anyone to help me. I shouldn't be worried about it. It was in God's hands. God would take care of them. But I wanted to take care of them myself without anyone standing in my way. This was something personal. I couldn't let it go.

As April was coming in, our neighbors, the Smiths, moved out a year before the attack. New neighbors moved in next door to us. They were also very nice and sweet people. The Carters had two girls. I love that we have there such good and friendly neighbors. One a rainy day in April, I was watching WWE when this spooky figure emerged from the shadows. They called him the Undertaker. I loved the way he beat his opponents. There was fear in his opponent's eyes. That's when I started to watching wrestling every week when he was on television. Diana and Paul never knew what I was thinking in my head.

On June 20, 1990, we wanted to go swimming because it was getting hot outside. Where we live, there was a pool at the top of the hill in the trailer park that used to be a farm. It had a silo and a barn. The whole family would spend the whole day up in a great little pool. For the time being, I forgot about what happened that night, to just be a kid for once and have fun. A lot of people spend their summer at the pool because it was free, but you had to pay for the food and drinks. After walking back home, Diana would cook dinner for all us while we were sleeping on the floor or the couch. Paul was in the kitchen, while Diana was cooking dinner. The television would be on and the air conditioner would be running.

By the time August arrived, Douglas and I were ready to head back to school. It was still hot but not as bad over the summer. There were days when it got over a hundred degrees. The one-year anniversary of that incident was coming. This time, I would be ready in case anything happens. Even though I am still a little nine-year-old boy, I wanted to get back at them. I tried not to let it bug me for the time being while I was at school. After the injury she suffered, it left a long scar, evidence of a lifelong trauma. I wish that it could have been me instead of Diana. I would have fought back, instead they chose a woman who couldn't fight because she was paralyzed in her right arm. Now I get anxious on Halloween. You have to be very careful with who you're dealing with when passing out candy.

September was approaching, and I was excited to be nine years old. The question was, who I was going to be dealing with if they came back what I have been told that the two masked figures was built. I wish I knew what they looked like. It's been almost a year and still no word from the police if they were caught or not. This year was going to be different. We were all was going to sit outside and wait. At that time, I was still going to church on Sundays even though I was still mad at God. I wanted to go anyway. As I got home from school that day, I went into my room. I just sat there doing nothing. On my free time at school, I was drawing pictures of graveyards and tombstones. I draw a picture of me burying the one who hurt Diana. I was just an angry young boy. I couldn't get over what happened to her. I was dealing with it pretty hard. I was the type of person who never showed my true emotions toward anyone. I would hide in a dark room, away from people. I didn't want anyone to see me like this, not even my own brother, or Paul, or Diana.

It was finally October. It's only been a year since the incident. We never knew what their intent was. They could have been trying to rob us, hurt us, or maybe even kill all of us. We were just happy they didn't kill Diana. They did hurt her enough that my parents were scared to pass out candy every year. It seemed they had this attack planned out I always thought they wanted to hurt or even kill someone that night.

On November 10, Diana's mom called to tell us that one of our relatives wasn't going to make through the night. She had cancer all over her body. Grandma told Diana that she would keep us updated throughout the night. By ten o'clock, we got a phone call saying our great-aunts passed away. We all had to wait till they got the funeral arrangement all set up. Diana's mom called the next day for the arrangements. It seemed like a family was getting hit hard by the devil, but we couldn't let him defeat us. We had to keep fighting, keep our chins up, and stay strong. I was still mad still from that Halloween night. The only thing I could do was keep fighting against the devil's attacks, but it was getting very hard to do it when I was very weak. Even though I was going to church every Sunday, my faith at that point was starting to weaken. We had the funeral services and burial the next day. The following night, we all came together to fight whatever was attacking us. We met up at Diana's mom's house. She invited us over for a barbecue and some games. We all took turns to ride the four-wheeler. We weren't going to let anything stop our family from having a great time, though we were still mourning over our great-aunt's passing. We all had to move on with to our lives.

As for me, I would go hide in the woods. At that time, I would just sit with a scowl on my face and stare off into the distance. I was in my own world. I didn't care to eat with everyone so I sit by myself, away from everyone else at the party. When they asked me if I was okay, I just smiled at them. I was letting the devil attack me because I was very fragile. I let my guard down, and it was eating me on the inside not letting anyone know I was mad. It was wearing me down slowly. I started harboring hate in me. All I cared about was horror movies and death. Well, the Hollywood horror movies were getting into my head. The Undertaker persona was starting to affect me, even though wrestling was fake. I knew his persona wasn't real. It was just his character, but they didn't called him the "man from the dark side" for nothing, which I didn't even know what it meant at the time.

In the early morning hours of December 20, we all went to church that Sunday even though I was mad at God. Church was making me feel good. I wasn't even thinking about anything at that moment except church. But it just seems like every time I was at home, bad feelings would come to my head. I wanted to talk with Paul and Diana about the situation, but I was too scared to talk about my problem. I didn't want anyone to know what I was actually thinking about. When Douglas was in his room, I was either in the living room or bedroom, watching horror movies or playing with my toys. One day, I was on in my room listening to Elvis Presley on the radio. Because I loved to listen to music, it kept my mind off everything. Grandpa Leroy loved Elvis.

4

Grandpa Leroy

On the morning of April the 28, 1991, a Saturday, Grandpa Leroy called mom and dad to say he would like to come to our place and have a barbecue. He said, "I can come over sometimes in May or June." Grandpa Leroy was a construction worker who had have to travel for his job. He told Diana that he would call in a couple of weeks to figure it out what day he would arrive. I always wanted to see my Grandpa Leroy, he was one my favorites.

Well, one nice sunny day, we got a phone call from Paul's mom. She told us that Grandpa Leroy was in a car accident. The police told her that an eighteen-wheeler knock him off the road. Paul's mom said he was rushed to the hospital. The truck was totaled and someone broke into his truck after the crash. Someone stole his tools and his money. We were all upset. Paul's mom told us that she would keep us informed as soon he arrives at the hospital. About five hours later, she reported that the doctors were going to run tests to see the damages he might have sustained during the accident. Diana called her mom and our preacher to pray for his recovery. About six hours later, we got the callback from Paul's mom. She told us they found a spot on his brain but the doctors didn't much till they ran more tests. Mom and Dad asked if we all can come down and see him. Paul's mom said, "I will ask the doctor if we all can. But all we can do now is just pray." We kept everybody up to date with what was going on with Grandpa Leroy. As we was about to head out the door to go grocery shopping, the phone rang, It was Paul's mom again telling us we can come down to see Grandpa Leroy. Diana asked if the doctor know what that spot was. She said they will find out tomorrow since the doctors went home for the day. So we all headed up there the next day. We were all very confused and sad. It hurt me to see my favorite grandpa was in the hospital. We had no answer besides what the doctors told us. For that night, we barely got any sleep we at all. We were so worried about him.

The next day, we went traveling to the hospital to see Grandpa Leroy. Diana turned on the radio and an Elvis song came on. We were all big Elvis fans, but the one song that bought me to tears, which I had to hide, was "If I Can Dream." Something about that song was telling me if this was really a dream or reality. As soon we got up to the hospital, Diana told us to be on our best behavior, "Or else you're not going to like when you see lying in the bed. He's in very bad shape." As soon we got up to the floor, the doctors came in to tell all of us that he a brain clot. It was too late, the damage was already done. They didn't think he would make it through the night. We all tried our best to be there for him. The doctors was going to put him into a medically induce coma. I was very sad to hear that. I told Diana, Paul, and grandma that I really love seeing him for Christmas and barbecues. That was about to be gone now.

Grandpa Leroy and I had a special relationship. I must have been one of his favorites, though he love Douglas too. It wasn't an easy thing for any of us, especially me. It crushed me on the inside. When we get into his room, he didn't look the same grandpa we were used to seeing. He always made the best barbecues. When he was awake, his eyes were on Douglas walking back and forth in the room. Then he would fall back in sleep. The doctors told us once again that they will run my more tests since he was in a very bad car accident. We didn't know what to expect for the weeks or months to come. Some of us stayed on the room with him, others went to the cafeteria, and the rest of our relatives went to the chapel to pray. It was a moment we had to leave up to God. It wasn't easy. The best way we could think of at this time was he could go home to meet his Maker. But it wasn't up to us or the doctors, it was up to God. All we could do was pray for the best. Later that day, we decide to go home. We were getting very tired. It was a long day. We have been there since 9:30 a.m. We wished him well and hoped he will get better as he kept staring at Douglas. His eyes never left my brother. He couldn't speak at all. We told Grandpa we will see him again tomorrow. As we were leaving, everybody else told him they will come back to see him. We all left together on the elevator. It was so quiet on that elevator. We all got into our cars and left at about 6:30 p.m. to go home and try to get a good night's sleep. As soon as we got home, Diana's mom called, asking about how grandpa was doing. Diana told her he was not doing good at all. The doctors feared he may pass away in the night. Diana's mom said the whole church was praying for him. Diana said, "Thanks, Mom, for all the prayers and support."

The next day at the hospital, the doctors told us that they found more bleeding in his brain. Paul's mom was in charging of Grandpa in case something happened to him. We all sat in his room, reminiscing on the memories we had with him. They ask if they could do surgery to reduce the swelling of his brain. Diana and Paul said they had to talk to his ex-wife, Paul's mom. Diana said, "I can give her a call." Diana went to the waiting room to call Paul's mom. They were on the phone for about forty-five minutes. When Diana came back in, she told the doctors that it was his wish to pass away peacefully. The doctors respected his wishes. It was so hard to see him like that so we decided to go out for some fresh air and get something to eat. Diana told Paul, "I'll meet you guys at the cafeteria. I'm going outside to smoke." Diana and Paul had been smoking since they were sixteen and seventeen years old. After that, we gathered the cafeteria as a family and ate dinner there. Diana didn't have to cook any dinner so we could just go home to take a bath and head straight to bed. We had church the next morning.

Paul's mom called to tell us to call her if anything happened so she can come over. Diana handed the phone to Paul so he can talk to his mom. When he got off the phone, he started crying. I went to my room and stayed there for the rest of the night. I laid my head on the pillow and closed my eyes. It had been a rough month for us. We just had to make the best of it. The very next day, Paul drove us to church but stayed at home in case the hospital called He picked us up after church. We decided to stay home too and rest and let the other relatives visit him. A couple of days later, we got another call from Paul's mom saying that he's not doing good at all. His blood pressure was dropping.

Grandpa was a fighter. He had his good days and bad days. He was indeed fighting. He wasn't going down without a fight. We just told her we will come over later on to see him. We left the house at around 2:30 p.m. It was a couple of days before Easter. It was getting tiring going up there a lot, but we wasn't going to stop seeing him. We were going to be there for him as much as we can. When got up to the hospital, Paul's mom was getting ready to leave for the day. We was supposed to stay for a little bit, but we were there for two and a half hours. We said we will be back on Easter Sunday. After church, we then headed up to the hospital. We were all very exhausted. Went spent half the day on Easter Sunday to visit him. He wasn't responding well. He was starting to get tired of fighting. Grandpa Leroy was indeed a Christian guy. We would see him at the grocery store or shopping at the local market. Losing him would be a big blow to our family. If we lost him, I would never get over that feeling. The very next day, he went into a coma and never came out of it. They doctors did one more test to see if the swelling went down. It was about the same.

The day after that, we were at the market to shop for groceries when the cell phone ring. Paul's mom broke the news to us that Grandpa Leroy went home to be with the Lord. At that moment, Paul rushed home. He didn't want to cry while driving. That was the hardest thing I had to deal with in my life. Grandpa was a strong believer in Jesus. He went to church every Sunday, although there were times he didn't because he had to work on a Saturday. The times we spent with him were great. Grandpa Leroy, Diana, and Paul always got along. They never fought or argue about anything. The staff at the hospital called all of us to come up and pay our final respects. Paul and Diana were crushed. I didn't want to see him like that myself. I was in my room for the rest of that day. As soon Paul went out to the store, the phone rang. Diana told her mom about Grandpa's passing. She said, "I would let the church know."

That next day, Paul's mom call to ask if she could to stay with us for three weeks. I was so excited to see my grandma, just after a death. About four hours later, Paul's mom pulled up in the driveway. Paul's mom didn't drive so she had a friend or a neighbor drive her everywhere she wanted to go. She said, "Sorry, we went out to lunch at McDonald's." Paul made a pot of coffee as we all gathered in the kitchen. Diana said that Grandma would take Douglas' room so me and my brother slept in my room. I slept on the floor and let Douglas take the bed. As the funeral arrangements was getting set up, we all drove to the local funeral home. Paul's mom, who was married to Grandpa Leroy, set up the arrangements. After we left the funeral home, we went to a little restaurant called the White Rose Café. It was a great place to eat. Then we went back home to watch television for the rest of the day. The funeral home called grandma to tell her she bring some clothes and other things to the funeral home tomorrow. It was so hard for her. She loved Grandpa Leroy to death. Even when they was divorce, she still loved him. The next day, we had to dive to his house to get the clothes he needed for the mortician to fix him up. By the time we got to the funeral home, his name was already on the board. The next few days were very hard for everyone, especially Paul's mom.

That day, me and Douglas were outside, playing with Hot Wheels. Now we always fought over the toys, like siblings always do, but we learned to share our toys with each. But throughout our playtime as kids, we never bothered our parents or Grandma when they was talking. That day was very foggy for early May. When it was a warm spring day, our parents would watch over us with the windows open. They were at the table drinking coffee. Diana, Paul, also Grandma loved to drink coffee in the afternoon. Diana called me and Douglas in for lunch. We all sat at the table and had lunch together as a family.

At the same time, I wondered why God was doing all this to me. I didn't know how God worked. I was really confused bout religious altogether. I was still young, not even eleven years old yet. Diana tried to sit down with me to tell how it works, but I wouldn't listen because of everything that happened.

On May 24, we went to the funeral home. Everyone who knew was there, even his coworkers. It was packed. Paul and Diana took us downstairs to the lounge to get a soda and some food that other people bought in for the family. The funeral did a nice job on Grandpa Leroy. We knew he was at peace with God. After the funeral home closed at 8:00 p.m., we went home and got ready for the burial tomorrow. We stayed up for about two hours and just talked about Grandpa Leroy till we got tried and went to bed.

The next day was a big day. The funeral wasn't till ten in the morning so we had time to take a shower and eat breakfast. My parents and Grandma had their coffee. Eventually, we all got dressed and got ready to head to the church for the funeral. Paul's mom said we should clean up the house and get rid of the stuff that we don't need after the funeral. Whey would all pitch in to clean the house. My brother Douglas and I were in school. Paul had to sit at home. But first thing first, we had a funeral to get to. We could worry about the house later. We all arrived at the church around 9:15 a.m. The only ones who were there was the pastor, the morticians, and the hearse. But we knew this was going to be a big funeral because Grandpa Leroy was well liked by everyone who knew him. It wasn't easy for any of us but we had to do it. We all entered the chapel to see him one last time. Grandma and Paul started tearing up. At around 9:45 a.m., people started gathering in the chapel for the funeral. There was still some time for some people to see him for the last time. Then promptly at ten o'clock, the pastor came up to the podium. Pastor Stacy told everyone in the crowed before we started the services that we were all going to pray. Afterward, the songs start playing. There were very beautiful hymns. Then Pastor Stacy got up and did the eulogy for Grandpa Leroy. The funeral went very well. After the last song was played, the pastor gave us an option to say our final goodbyes before they shut the lid on the casket. The whole room was waiting to see him for the last time. By the time we were all done, we walked out of chapel while the pallbearers carried the casket out to the hearse.

When the casket was loaded into the hearse, the police was positioned in front of the hearse. The pastor and funeral director told us if we are going to the cemetery, we need to turn our flashers and blinkers on. As we were driving out of the church parking lot and unto the highway, the police had to stop traffic. That was a very touching moment. Everybody was paying their respects. At the cemetery, we waited till the pallbearers got there. We stood at the end of the hearse when they took out the casket to his gravesite. That's when everybody knew this was really our last time to see him ever again. Now we just have his memories. The pastor said one last thing before we prayed over the casket and said our last goodbyes.

A day after the funeral, Diana, Paul, and Grandma decided to wait a couple of days before we cleaned up his house. We were still in mourning and wanted to take time for one another. That Saturday, May 27, Paul dropped off Diana and his mom to clean out the house. The only problem was what they were going to do with all those cats he took care of. They were thinking of giving them to the humane society to give them up to good homes. So on the first day, they got rid of a lot of stuff, but it took them a few weeks to get rid of everything. After a week, Paul was helping clean it out. He had to be back at around two thirty to wait for the bus to drop us off at three. It was a lot of driving back and forth every day, but it worked out great. After six to seven weeks, they finally got everything out of the house. We kept some stuff but had to throw away a lot because we didn't need it.

After months and months, it felt different somehow with no phone calls or visit. This bothered me a lot because I was so close to him. Christmas 1991 was coming up. We had to try to move on from his death. That's what he would have wanted us to do. When Christmas finally came around, we knew he wasn't around to call us anymore. That first Christmas without him changed things for me completely.

5

The Cult

In the beginning of the school year 1998, Douglas and I were getting older. I was now fourteen years old and Douglas was twelve. I would be starting high school in a year. In gym class one day, we were playing volleyball indoors because it was raining outside. I had so much fun gym class. It was one of my favorite classes in school, along with history. Well, I was reaching for the volleyball so it wouldn't drop and give the other team a point. My friend Jake stepped on my pinkie finger and broke it by accident. I was actually mad at him. After getting an X-ray, it showed a crack. I had to go see a specialist to see if I needed surgery or not. After returning to school that following day, I wanted to get into his face and started yelling at him. Well, the teacher heard it, waltzed into the room, and said, "Sit down right now, all of you!" I didn't want to sit down at all. I wanted to continue telling at him for breaking my finger. I wasn't going to be able to do gym for the next seven weeks. I was really upset and very disappointed about it. My anger was building up. I was starting to dislike my classmates. The next couple of weeks, I would have to see a specialist. The good thing was no surgery was required. That was a big break there. God was healing my finger so that I didn't surgery, but I was still pretty angry at my classmate for breaking it.

We was about to be on spring break in 1998. Mom and Dad picked us up from school. There was a time in school where I was bullied by other students. This time, I wanted to fight them, though

I didn't know how. Should I do it on school property or off, where I wouldn't get caught and suspended. I was constantly angry on the inside. I would get home, go straight to my room, and hide there or take a nap. I would feel a lot better when I woke up to have dinner with the rest of my family. We all sat down together and ate like a family. Diana and Paul told us we would be going to summer school and vacation Bible school during summer vacation. I really didn't want to do vacation Bible school. I wanted to stay with my parents. I was starting to lose connection with God and the church more and more. I was getting tired of hearing about God. Starting ninth grade, it didn't get any better. It just got worse in my four years of high school. While my brother Douglas was in vacation Bible school, I just stayed home and watch a bunch of horror movies and the Undertaker on television.

Vacation Bible school lasted for a week. We would have to go shopping to get some school supplies and haircuts. Our last stop was going out to dinner. Diana didn't feel like cooking anything since it was late in the day. By the time got home, we had to take our bathes and brush our teeth. We got to stay up for a little while and watch television. So the following, day we decided to do something fun before we started school in August. Diana couldn't work anymore after her surgery and getting attack by two masked men. On June 28, we saw fireworks at the park at night. It was a fun time. During Fourth of July, we usually set up fireworks.

I got ready to go back to school now with big teens. We had to go up to the school to meet our teachers and find out what classes I was going to be in. I was in a lot of special education class and in a couple of normal classes. I also had some great teachers and met some new people. I was still getting picked on and attacked by teens. That was my life in school. I wanted to hurt someone to show them I wasn't going to deal with the bullying this year, but I didn't though. On August 15, 1998, the first day of school, I got picked on a lot. But I in the first two days, we had no homework, which was great. Going back to school, we all had to listen to the rules. I was never one like to listen to anyone because of the way I was treated. I was sitting by myself never really wanted to have anything to do with anyone. Now there were some new faces at school that year. I don't know if they transferred schools. I never saw those guys before. For some reason, there were days they all wore black clothes. There were other days when they wasn't dress in black, but a one of girl always wore black finger nail polish and eyelash all the time. I just sat there looking at her. I thought, Well, maybe that's what she like to wears. Who knows? It's none of my business. If she wanted to come up and start talking to me, I will talk to her back.

One day in early September, that same girl sat next to me and started talking to me. She asked me if I believe in God. I told her yes but I was really mad at him. I asked her if she believe in God. She responded, "I am into Wicca." At that point, our conversation ended. She never asked me if I would like to join, but she seemed friendly. The next few months, she told me she had a guy friend that was into devil worshipper. Those guys were really deep into that stuff. I never Told Diana and Paul about this teenager. However, I did research on it. At first, I thought, *I hope this girl don't talk me into it.* Her friend went to school with us. One time in the hallway, she came up to me with her friend. She introduced me to him. He told me his name was Fred. I didn't know anything about them, only that they were into these dark magic stuff. As long they didn't drag me into it, I didn't worry. At the back of my mind though, I what happened to Diana on Halloween and all the horror movies were beginning to affect me. I was thinking about it more and more every day. I hiding it from everybody. I could either get right with God or let the devil take over me. At that point, I didn't know what to do with my life. I was an easy target for anyone to talk to me getting me into some kind of group. However, after I read what they did, I couldn't get into it.

By early spring, school went well so far. I met different kinds of teenagers who didn't believe in God or go to church. I always believe in God, but this young girl and guy was changing that for me. One day at lunch, I had to try not to pay any attention to them. They were very creepy. For the rest of that day, I went from class to class and buried myseff in my studies. The only time I would see them was either in the halls or lunch room. I didn't have any classes with them. My parents never knew who they were. I always kept that to myself. When I went home, I just go to my room. When Diana and Paul asked me how my day was, I said, "Just fine."

The very next day, I would not see that young men and women. They weren't at school. Either they were sick or skipped school. One of their friends came up to me. He seemed very normal, but I don't know if I could trust him. He did tell that he went to church and believe in God. That took a lot of the pressure off me. He told me to overlook his friends, they were just weird. I took his word, but I really didn't speak to him too much. He was pretty quiet. I was also pretty quiet. I didn't really say much in school. I only talked if the teacher asked me a question. The months went by, and the couple was there off and on for a short period of time. They really didn't mind skipping school or playing hooky for once. I was left alone for a while. No one came up to me. I was just sitting there at the table while everyone else were eating lunch. Students at my school were preppy. I didn't care for those kind of people. I was just trying to mind my own business.

It was that time of year. We were always worried what Halloween was going to be like for us every year. We weren't going to take any chances. My only fear was, what if they weren't done and want finish what they did to Diana seven years ago. They already messed our family up. We could never ever get back what they took from us. But I was actually celebrating what happened seven years ago because I still was trying to track and hunted them down my ego and my madness in me was hurting me of not letting what happen go I wanted to do something to mess up whoever gets in my way or whoever hurts my family.

The next day, I saw the young couple at school. Something change in me. I decided to get more information about what they do. They said they could induce me to some friends but suggested I should go home and think about it for as long as I needed to see if I wanted to meet one of their people. They told me to think it over while on Thanksgiving break. Well, Thanksgiving was getting closer and I had been doing some thinking, but I was still wasn't sure what I want to do. I was never an atheist, but I was pissed off at God. I would change to something scarier and more frightening I joined these people. I would target those who bullied me and picked on me. I was going to show God I wasn't afraid of him or anyone else. But after Thanksgiving, I told them I still needed time to think about it. I didn't know what I could get myself into at all so I had to do a lot of research on the cult. On a Saturday afternoon, I was watching World Wrestling Federation. The lights went out and the Undertaker came out. They had another nickname for him, the Man from the Dark Side. Then all the sudden, my brain clicked. There was a way I could destroy my enemies.

After the holidays, on March 16, a group of representatives from the amusement park in St. Louis came to our school. They were hiring people. I stood in line to put in an application. They told me when to come out for my interview. The creepy girl was putting in her application too. I never thought anything about it. Maybe her boyfriend told her to stalk me or maybe she just wanted a spring or summer job out there. After school, I went home and told Paul and Diana I got a job interview on March 26. I was sixteen years old and about to have my first job ever. I was going to see what the real world was like. It was scary but I would finally have my own money to spend. Diana and Paul said it was okay to have the job and sat down with me to talk to me about having a savings account and a checking account. After that following Saturday, I got the job. So I was working on weekends. It wasn't a full-time job till school was out. Just a couple of days later, right before I started working at amusement park, I told the creepy couple I would be working there. The guy told me that his girlfriend also got the job. I thought they were keeping something back from me but no idea what. After school in Thursday, Diana and Paul took me to the bank to open a checking and savings account. I would be getting paid every week now, however, Diana and Paul put some changes in the bank to keep it open.

School was out for the weekend when I finally started my first job. The first day went very well. I made new friends but also got picked on by one young man. He didn't like the music I was listening to. I looked at him and told him to just shut up and back off. Then I walked away after that and just worked till my supervisor told me to take a lunch break. It was warm but not hot so I went on my lunch break at noon. I met this guy who was a little older than me. He introduced himself as Gary. We sat across from each other at the table. I really didn't know what to say. The girl from school also sat with us also but didn't really talk much. Gary told her that she was welcome to chat with us. I told Gary I knew her from school. But she don't talk much only me and her boyfriend. At that point, I thought, *Why aren't you talking?* She was lying to him. I just covered up for her, that's all. After I was done eating, I said, "I'll talk to you guys later," but then she also stood up and walked with me. I was thinking, *Why is she following me everywhere I go?* I really didn't have time to ask her because I had to get back to work. Everything was going well for me. I enjoying work at the theme park, it just so much fun. Then once I got off work, Paul picked me up and asked me how work was. I said it was great and fun. I really didn't talk much because I was too tired. I just wanted to go home, eat dinner, and get ready to work again on Sunday.

The very next day, Paul drove me to work. He said, "Maybe it's time for you to get your permit." For some reason, I was always scared to drive. It was a cloudy day and likely going to rain. I was working on grounds at that time. There wasn't too many people out in the park because it was pouring all day so my supervisor came up and told me I could clock out. I was working about four and a half hours so I clocked out and had lunch. Then I stayed to watch television in the employees' restaurant (Yeah, we had own lunch spot to eat without guests bugging us). Around five, I called Paul to have him pick me up from work. He told me he would be out there in about thirty minutes. I thanked and hung up.

Some of the crew I worked with never did like me. I just wanted to be accepted. I never bothered anyone so I have no idea why they didn't like me. I always tried to get along with everyone. No one knew I had problems. I was hoping and praying that I would get through my first year of work without any problems. Now my coworkers would called me names like "four-eyes" and "gay" just because I like a boy bands. I wasn't gay and I like all kinds of music. At that time, some of the employees talked behind my back. It was hurtful, but in my mind, I knew that there were just trying to make a monster out of me. I already had anger issues, and they were just poking me to make things worse for me. I tried to ignore them and walk away from it. It was hard enough getting bullied in school where no one would stand up for me. Once I go back to school in the fall, I thought about getting revenge on those students. I was getting very tired of the name-calling and bullying. The girl I worked with at Amusement park told them to knock it off and threatened to hurt anyone that would try to hurt me. Her boyfriend had a mean streak in him. It was scary to see him pissed off. They asked me if I would like to join their group in the first five months off school. I didn't want to join because they wouldn't leave me alone at all. It was nice for them to stick up for me in amusement park though.

I didn't hang out with Gary after amusement park closed down for the wintertime. He and I were Christians, but I was not currently going to church. I also told I didn't wanted to have anything to do with God and I wasn't going to say anything else. I remember him telling me that when the park was open during the summertime, tenth grade wasn't going to be better. But it was only getting harder and harder for me. I was so ready to be out of school for good. The new year was coming. A new era was approaching in 2000. I had one more year of studies left before the school year ended. I would be in eleventh grade and Douglas would be in ninth grade. I was excited to go to my junior prom by next April. On spring break, I was back at amusement park once again. This year, there were different people working there, but the same girl who asked me to join their group was still out there. It distracted me in school. I really had a hard time concentrating on work a lot of times. My mind was not focused at work half of the time. My thoughts revolved around harming someone, but I kept that quiet while I was at work. I couldn't fight every security guard if someone picked a fight with me, and I wouldn't be able to fight the police either because they could tase or pepper spray me. Anyone who picked a fight or provoked me, I would beaten that person. I would be arrested and go to jail. Then I would have had to answer Paul and Diana and give them am explanation for my actions. So I just had to keep my mouth shut and listen to the supervisor or my leader. I was starting to build up hate in my life. I seemed that the girl and her boyfriend were watching me to see how I would respond if I ever did get angry. Every time I actually got mad, I would black out. It was very scary. Any little thing would make me mad. Whether you were just eating or drinking, I would get angry. I started avoiding people as much as I can at school and at work.

When July came, there was an event called Fright Fest. I told Diana and Paul I wanted to attend. They allowed me to go. I was pretty excited about this event. I was doing grounds for a county fair at amusement park one day when I told Gary that I was planning to join Fright Fest organized by the company JPM, a production company from Atlanta, Georgia. I quit working for amusement park just to work for this company. It was the greatest event that I ever worked for. I also worked at the other haunted house. I was dressed up as Ghostface when a little boy came walking up toward me. I popped out from behind the wall and scared the little boy. He punch me in the face and ran away. It was an accident and I still had a job to do. Security saw what happened and stayed with me till first aid came to check me out. I had a bruised cheek but they told me nothing was broken. They told me to clock out and go home, and the supervisor thank me for a job well done. Besides getting punch during Halloween, I took home a great check. I enjoyed doing. I would have done it again in a heartbeat.

6

Evil

In 2000, I went to my junior prom with the theme "Titanic." It was a great theme. The following year would be my final year of high school and my last prom. As soon everyone graduates, we will probably never see each other anymore. When I worked at Walmart though, I would see some of my former classmates. I was actually very excited about the new year, the first time I have been happy in a while. It didn't last that long. Now it was time for me to plan my future. Unfortunately, my life would take a turn for the worse. I got suspended for two days from fighting. I knocked this boy off the stool because he bullied me. He got up to punch me. I knock him back down again. The worse part about the situation was suspended for five days to my two days. That night, we got a call from Diana mom's who told her that her dad passed away at the age of seventy-two. I didn't care for the guy that much, but he passed away in September 2000.

My last of school wasn't peaceful. I finally would got some payback at some of my classmates for bullying all these years. My temper would get out of hand, my nightmares were getting worse, and my behavior was getting weird and very strange. I will still searching for the man who responsible for the pain they caused my mom, my family, and especially me. I never stopped looking for the two men who attacked my mom. I was going to hunt them down. I was watching more and more horror movies. I was also watching more of the Undertaker.

When I was fifteen or sixteen, my mom told me that Paul wasn't my real dad. It almost drove me over the edge. I wanted to blow up right there in front of mom and Paul. That's when I wanted to track down Jason and make him pay dearly for what he has done to us. I was told that fact two years before I graduated from school. I was starting to hang out with the creepy couple and their friends. I wanted to find some way to put this pain behind me. I never forgot what my mom told me about Jason. I wanted to tell my new friends about him. I was trying to look for a way out but I couldn't. It was starting to bug me as time went on, but this was personal matter between me and Jason. I wanted to deal with him my way, if I ever caught up to him. Diana thought it would be best not to look for him, but I wanted to look for him as badly as the two masked men. In the meantime, I put everything else behind me to get through prom and graduate.

At lunch one day, I was sitting with some of my classmates but didn't talk to them. I just ate my lunch and waited till the bell rang for class. I didn't want to tell any of my friends what was bugging me. During Miss Speck's class, she told us to pick out a job that we would like to do out of high school. I spoke up and said funeral director. One of my classmates said, "You're the Deadman!" I turned around to look at him and said, "That's what they called the Undertaker on WWE." He said, "Well, that has something to do with the Dead," I thought, *Okay, I take it.* I went to the library and started to research on how to become a funeral director. I went on to the computer and found a school about an hour away from me. I type in to get information from the school they send it in the and I got about a week after I sent them my address and it was pretty interesting. I thought, *That's the job I want after college.*

When I got home, I told my mom and Paul that I wanted to be a mortician. Shocked, they said, "Come again?" I repeated that wanted to be a mortician and work on dead people. The first question that came out of their mouth was, "Why would you want to work with dead people? Plus we don't have the money to send you to college." Both my parents couldn't work at all now since they were disabled. I was still working at amusement park. Paul would have to drive me back and forth to college because my mom couldn't drive with her paralyzed her left arm. I didn't take thir rejection too well. I got very upset and disappointed. They asked me how I was going to pay for college. I answered with student loans and a Pell Grant. They said, "Well, you're not going to have the money to pay it back. With a Pell Grant, you don't have to pay back at all." The next day, I did a paper on being a funeral director. When I turned the paper in the following week, I got an A-plus. But the problem was trying to convince my parents to let me go to college. I went down to the army and national guard recruiting stations. I passed everything excepted math, which I was never good in. I wanted to make something out of my life and do a good deed but nothing worked out as I wanted it to. That really upset me.

Prom was just a few weeks away. I asked my parents if I should I get a tuxedo or wear one of my suits to prom this year. Diana said, "Wear one of your suits." Okay, I can deal with that one. The next day, I started to look for a date for prom. In the first two months, I didn't have any luck at all so I asked one of my friends, Patty. She said yes. I went home and told my parents I had a date for prom, one of our neighbors. They said, "Cool. We want a lot of pictures of you guys together." On prom night, I was so nervous and excited. I went up to her house for pictures. Then I took her to our house where my mom took a picture of us. Paul drove us to prom. We went inside and posed for pictures. After we got them done, I told Patty, "Let's go find our seats." A moment later, she said, "I need to go to the bathroom. I will be back in five to ten minutes." I said, "Okay, sounds good." I waited patiently for her to come back. Five minutes later, she didn't show up. I waited for another five minutes. She still hasn't come back so I decided to look for her. I was about to walk out of the gym when someone came up to me and said, "I saw your date leave." It was very embarrassing. I had no words, I was so angry and mad about the whole thing. It ruined my whole night. I didn't have any fun at all. I just sat at the table, hanging my head down. I didn't want anyone to hear me cussing under my breath. After a few deep breaths I decide to call Paul and Diana to pick me up from prom. When they asked me what's wrong, I said nothing. They knew I was upset. For a very long time, I never got over that. I thought I wanted revenge on her. I wanted to mess with her mind, just like she did me, but it was hard for me to get revenge on her. The next day at school, we walked past each other in the hallways, never speaking to one another. I never talked to her again for the rest of high school. I wasn't happy about anything that was going on with my life.

In the next few weeks before graduation, I had to prep myself for the big day. We went on our senior trip and had a lot of fun. I didn't really wanted to do it at all I just wanted to stay into a dark room and hide. It was so hard for me to even speak to one of my classmates. All I did was think of evil, not putting God in my life at all. He already made me so unhappy. Before we graduate, we had to have rehearsals. We did the first time right. The night before graduation, there were some pretty bad storms. The next day, while we were waiting for our diplomas, a really bad lightning storm started. Eventually, everyone came up to get their diplomas then we threw our hats in the air. Finally, the rain poured down so hard, I lost the tassel on my hat. We all went to the cafeteria to see everyone for the last time. I didn't think it was going to be very hard for me once I got out. Afterward, we went to our local YMCA and stayed up the whole night. I was pretty tired. That following morning, we went back to high school to get our final awards I was glad school was over. I didn't have to deal with anyone else's crap. Mom and Paul came to pick me up from the school. I just went home and slept until four in the afternoon. I was very tried and exhausted from that night.

On September 11, 2001, I got up at about seven. We had to go over to the school for a meeting with the principle regarding my brother. We turned the television on till Mom got up to get ready for the meeting. The news broke that the World Trade Center was hit by a small aircraft. We saw a live stream of the building on fire. I told Paul that was that was a big plane that hit the building, a small plane won't do that much damage. So around 8:20 a.m., before the Mom got up out of bed, we saw a second plane hit the building. Paul and I gasped, "Oh crap!" Mom asked, "What's going on?" We told her that America was under attack. She got up right away. We had no idea what was going on so we drove quickly to the school. They told us that the Pentagon had just been hit as well. After what happened to our country, I walked up to the national guards facility. There was nothing there. It resembled a ghost town. There were no cards or people running around. Everyone was at home, glued to their television. It was very scary. So I went back home to keep up with the event on television. Watching the aftermath, it was just so sad and horrible. Why would people would do that? Just a few months later, I moved on. After a year, I started to track down the two masked men that assaulted Diana on Halloween night. I wasn't going to give up trying to find them. I couldn't let it go at all. If I had to search the darkness to find them, I will. If only God would hear my prayer and find these two men, I wouldn't have been so mad at him. I would have moved on with my life.

By 2003, I have been out of high school for two years. I wanted to get into the military. I went back to work at amusement park the next day. I have been there for three years. My brother got a job out there but didn't stay long. He met a girl who would become his wife. Her name was Jennifer. I thought they looked great together, and they both went to each other's proms. Though I never stop believing in God, I was starting to have trust issues. I walked around with a look like I was going to beat you or hunt you down. My attitude was changing and starting to freak people out. I wasn't acting like I was tough, but I wasn't going to let anyone bring me down anymore or bully me for any reason. I wasn't acting like myself. Everything was starting to boil over. I was ready to start attacking anyone who got in my way. I wasn't feeling apologetic or show anyone any mercy whatsoever. My attitude was changing in front of my parents. They still couldn't get anything out of me. I would get up every morning and go to bed at night all mad and pissed off. It was pretty scary for my family, and it was taking a toll at work also.

I passed out one time. It was so hot that I fainted twice. They had to take me to first aid and had me lie down on the bed till they got hold of my parents. They came and pick me up. My parents had to call my doctor to let him what was going on with me. The next day, I went to the doctors. They had to put a heart machine on me and told me to come back in one week to find out the results of the test. Well, that following week, I went back but they told me it would be a couple days to read it. Well, the doctor called me the following week and told me I had an unregular heartbeat. A week later, I went back to work with a doctor's note saying I can take a break and that I need to be careful working out in the sun. Well, one supervisor didn't like that I need to take a break. He told me the next time he saw me resting, he was going to write me up. Well, I didn't take to kindly to that remark. He opened the floodgates. We both started arguing. I yelled at him and told him I quit. Then I called my parents. They picked me up asked me what's wrong. I told them I wanted to open the gates of hell, throw him in, and let his skin and flesh come off. I never went back in 2003. He was making me more angry. I wasn't going to let him win this battle. I was out for revenge. At that point, I had a lot of hatred in me. Since I quit amusement park, I worked at another job in Hardee's. The supervisor there she was no better cussing out her employee's and guest that came to eat there.

I let this couple talk me into joining their group, which I should never let them do. They got into my head, it wasn't even funny at that point. I was just very mad at the whole world. I was going to find every way to destroy people with the madness and hatred inside me. I quit Hardee's after three days because of the supervisor's behavior. I went to work at the local Walmart for six months. I had so much trouble focusing on my job. I was more worried about hurting other people. A woman who works at Walmart told me on our lunch break that she was in witchcraft and Wicca. I told her I was so mad at God. I also disclosed that had a group of friends that does devil worshipping and they told me how to burn the cross upside down. I wanted to put the pentagram at the police department and watch it burn to the ground. I added that I would love to hang out with her sometime.

The managers at Walmart told me to get help. I just ignored them, not paying any attention to them. They kept trying to talk with me but it wouldn't get through my head. They had to call my parents to talk with the head manager at Walmart. My parents asked me what I did. I just kept quiet. So they said, "Well, we are just going to get the information from them." At the meeting in the office of the Walmart manager, he told my parents I was creeping out all the employees. I told them I was going to lit dark candles and bring some evil things up. The manger then said, "The boy needs some help." At that point, no knew what was going on in my life all. I was falling apart. It was starting to scare my parents and everybody around me. It wasn't a pretty picture at all. My parents took me home. I was at Walmart only for eight months. It was going to be a long struggle and take a lot of work to get me back to my normal self.

On May 22, 2004, Paul and I got into an argument outside on the porch. He was alcoholic. We didn't know why he was drinking so much. When drunk, he would get mean and cuss. I went over to his car and kick it. Then I went to my room and punched a hole in the wall. When I went back out, one of the neighbors called the police. They warned that the next time they came down there, one of us was going to jail. They told me to just go for a walk. I didn't listen. About twenty minutes later, we got into it again. The police came back down. This time, they took me to jail, the first of many. The last time, the police took both me and Paul to jail. I got sent up twenty hours each time to calm myself down, and there was never any chargers filed by the state of Missouri or my parents.

When I got out of jail, I kept hanging out with the same friends. I took the whole thing to the next level. My parents were now in danger of losing me completely. I was going to end up dead or in prison for good. They told me they would have me committed to the hospital. I told them, "I was going to run so none of you could find me or anything." I wanted to run away from my problems.

One day, I was still sleeping when they went out. When they got back, I was out of bed. When I asked them where they went, they didn't tell me anything till the police arrived to take me to the hospital. I got so mad, I started cussing at them. I told them, "I am sending you both to hell!" Well, they didn't take too kindly to that at all. I fought the police but they handcuffed me in the front and dragged me d to the hospital. When I got there, a cop pated me on my shoulder and told me good luck. I knew from the start that I had a big problem, but I never said anything about it to anyone. I just kept it quiet. In the next few days, I never knew anything about what my parents and the doctors were planning on the phone or otherwise in private. My parents came down to see me a few days later. The doctors told my parents they will release me in about a week. When they release me from the hospital, they told me I had to take my meds the doctor prescribed, but I didn't take them. My parents were in a tough spot. They tried everything, their backs were against the wall, and they didn't know what else to do with me. However, now they knew something my diagnosis, though they never told me what it was. The next thing was try to get me away from the people that were putting things into my head that provoked me to act out and make bad decisions.

It was now getting hard for Diana and Paul. They were running out of options. They found a company that would get me out Union, Missouri, but I continued to act out. I was hiding in the dark room; it was getting very weird for everyone around me. One day, Paul was drinking again. We both got mad at each. I threw him of the porch, which shattered his ankle. He had to have screws and plates in his ankle for the rest of his life. They thought about calling the police but eventually opted out because they were protecting me. I regret that to this day. I couldn't forgive me myself for what I put my family through.

Eventually, I managed to go back work to an amusement park in 2004 I only stayed there for about four months. I got blamed for something I never did, causing me to lose my job. I was mad as hell. At that time, I wanted to go after the workers who framed me. Now I didn't have a job so I stayed home till my parents found somewhere else for me to go to be safe. My neighbor who knew my real dad Jason took me to his family farm, trying to help out my parents. It didn't work out either. My neighbor wasn't mad. I think he knew something was going on. He thought that the WWE wrestler Undertaker had a bad influence on me. He didn't care to watch that stuff. Everyone around me, not even my parents, was trying to be nice to me because I always found a way to put them through all sorts of hell. Now I was wearing black clothes with my new Goth friends.

7

New Beginnings

On November 14, 2003, Mom and Paul wanted me to go into a group home. They needed me to get out of Union, Missouri. They thought it was for the best for me and for them. My parents wanted someone to get me under control and get me away from my friends' bad influence. It wasn't safety for me to live in Washington, Indiana, anymore. They found a company that would take me in and try to get my behavior back on track. They were planning to have me move out in spring of 2004. Paul had surgery on his shattered foot on March 20, 2004.

    The only way I could escape the temptation of evil was to try to start a new life elsewhere. I was still watching the horror movies and the Undertaker. I didn't want to leave at all. I took all the nightmares and the evil with me to the detriment of the next people I came in contact with. They had to deal with the same stuff as my parents did. I was a nightmare for years and years to come. No one knew what they were getting themselves into. We went to meet people from life skills class. When we arrived at that meeting, all hell broke loose between me and mom as soon as we got started. Paul and the people from life skills were shouting and cussing at everybody. Diana and Paul never told anyone that I had post-traumatic stress disorder (PTSD) or anxiety disorder. I felt like my parents left me with compete strangers. I don't know why no one ever told me and the life skills people.

So I started living in the home with two other guys. Things took a turn for the worse again. Sometimes it got very intense, but I would always hide in my room. Whenever I could, I didn't want to eat lunch or dinner with the two guys. I just wanted to hide and complete darkness from everyone. I wanted to get back to church and read my Bible, but at the same time, I couldn't let go of whatever I was dealing with. I wanted to hang on to whatever it was that kept me struggling. The two guys and staff witnessed me acting like horribly. I wish I could just stop and live a normal life. There was plenty of times when I threated the staff, it almost escalated into a fistfight between me and one of the guys. I was a deeply messed-up young men. As I moved from one home to another, they were starting to lose control of me. When they told me to go for a walk, I told them to "go to hell." I did try a couple of times to go back to church. I was happy to go back, but then at night, I would get in my aggressive moods. I wanted this to be a new beginning for me. When they would take me to the doctor for a checkup, I would fight the doctors. I knew right there I should stop. I reflected on how many people I put through hell to make myself feel good.

I wasn't happy being there. At times I wouldn't come out of my room and hide from the world. I knew the staff had to be tough on me and keep doing what they were doing. There was one staff I liked. He was such a great man. His name was Jose. He never done me wrong. He knew I was going through something. Don't get me wrong, there was a couple of people I like to chat or hang out with, but almost all of them treated me like crap. Finally, I move to another house in 2005. I wanted to go back to school. I went to my local college in Union, Indiana, where I took classes to be a funeral director. I've always wanted to be one since I was little. I faced my fears of dead people after my first semester of college I got all *A*s and had 4.0 GPA. I was very happy with those grades. I went back the following year to some more classes. It was very important for me to have these classes because being a funeral director required twenty-eight credits to be licensed.

I was pretty much in denial about everything. I had to figure a way out to get back into God's hand. Do I just keep doing the things

I am doing, get into trouble with the law some more, and just keep putting up a fight against God? I believe I was still under the devil's spell to do bad things. I knew that if I fought against God, he would punish me for everything I have done to him, plus God is more powerful than the devil. I was very thankful for the friends I had. In 2005, my struggles with good and evil continued at that point in my life. I was not a very nice guy at all. Everyone who knew me saw the hurt in my eyes. We just had to figure out how to go by getting me to my life prior to when I was a kid. The only person who could change me was me. Before I could even get better for myself and for my friends, I would have to seek some help. I just didn't know how to go asking for that help. I was very shy with talking about my life to other people. I didn't have any trust or faith. It was harder to even attend church with the way I was, however, I told myself I would go. But as Sundays rolled around I never went. I was lying to myself all that time. Church was not going to hurt me or nothing, but I was afraid I would be judged for the way I was. I never dated either because I didn't want the women to know I was living a double life. My ego was controlling me so much it was just like I was in a daze for a long time. I was still going to school, but I wouldn't talk to anyone at the college or at work.

One afternoon in the spring of 2006, I went to apply at the YMCA for a custodian job. I met the supervisor, Eric Thompson. He was nice at first, but I heard not so great things about him. I never really knew him. Eric had two jobs, one at the YMCA and he was also in a band. Eric and I never got along during the eight years I was there. But just a couple of months into my new job, my boss Eric was starting to get under my skin, putting me down and calling me names. I didn't know how I dealt with him for eight years. There were times I just wanted to tell him, "You're messing with the wrong guy," but if I did that, I would got fire.

Also in 2006, a new Batman movie came out called *Batman Begins*. I have always been a big Batman fan. I watched that movie over a thousand times now. In the middle of the movie, Bruce Wayne was caught leaving a hotel by Rachel. I give credit to Christopher Nolan and David S. Goyer for the quote Rachel said in the movie,

"It's not who you are underneath, it's what you do that defines you." That quote was something I needed to hear. I didn't let that sink till about seven years after I've seen the movie again. Toward the end, Rachel told Batman she would like to know his name because he might die. Batman gave her the same line she told Bruce. That quote from *Batman Begins* was inspiring to me. There was a reason for that quote. Maybe that was something God wanted me to hear.

On July 25, 2007, my sister-in-law found out that she was pregnant. We didn't know yet if it was a little boy or girl, but we were all very excited that I was going to be a uncle and my parents were going to be grandparents. I was actually happy that day when I went to work and told everyone I was going to be an uncle. Diana told me that my sister-in-law was having morning sickness. We wouldn't find out the gender of the baby till maybe about September or October. We were going to have a new edition to our family. I really needed to change my life around the baby who was going to be born sometime in March 2008. Diana kept me up to date about the pregnancy. In just a couple of months, God is about to put a little baby in our lives that we will never forget. Finally in March, the baby could come at any time. We were ready for the newborn. Then one day while I was at work, I got a phone call from Diana. I had to wait till I went on my lunch break to call back. When I called my mom, she told me that Erica had her baby, and they name him Ethan Ray. They had the name already pick out but didn't want to say anything till they were sure that's what they wanted to name him. I didn't get to see him till he came home. He was everyone's pride and joy.

One cold winter day, Eric asked me how my day was. I didn't really care for the guy at all. Eric was just too cocky after telling him about the exciting news of my soon-to-be nephew's arrival. He wouldn't say one word toward me and his staff. He was never polite to anyone, except maybe to his friends from his band.

I was just waiting till I get myself back on track and get myself a woman. I did go on these dating sites, but a lot of the women were just not for me. If I did meet someone, I didn't know how it would work because I wasn't even ready for a woman, plus I was still into this paranormal stuff like ghost hunting. I shouldn't be messing with that stuff since I left the cult.

In the middle of June, my mom got a call from her mom. She told Diana that her brother was not doing well. He been sick and been in and out of the hospital. My grandma kept my mom up to date then she would call me to let me know what was going on with him. Then in September 2008, he was back on the hospital from a heart attack. He was overweight and had poor health. On March 16, 2009, my uncle passed away. I was working that day when I got the tragic news. It was sad, but my mom had a secret she never said till after the funeral. She told me that my uncle once pulled a gun to her head, which I never knew before. Once again my family was all about secrets. My mom went to her brother's funeral, but I didn't know how she felt about his death. She never talked about it after it went down. Diana told me he did stupid things in life when he was young. I never got to saw him over the last three years because he lived in Farmington, Indiana. We didn't get to see him that much. Diana said he worked at the stadium for the Cardinals.

One day while I was working at the YMCA, a new guy was starting work there. He seemed like a good person, just very kind and very friendly. At first, I was going to induce myself to him, but Eric brought him over to me. Eric said, "This is Daniel." I said, "Hi, nice to meet you." He told me his name was Nick. I said I liked his name, and he thanked me. We got along just fine. I knew we were going to become very good friends. I told myself that if he can help me with my struggles, I would love to talk to him about it sometime, but I didn't want to tell him about my problems yet. At lunch, we both sat across from each other and made jokes. Eric came by and asked us what we were laughing about. We didn't tell him it was about him. We were very loud and making jokes about him. Right before we left, Nick asked, "Would you like to hang out sometime?" He said he had a friend he would like me to meet. I told him not to talk about God. When he asked why, I told him about my past but didn't really get into all the details. I said, "I'm just mad at him right now." He tried to get me to look at the positive side of all the stuff that happened in my life, but I didn't really listen to him at all. I just let it go in one ear and out the other. Then he said, "I won't force you, but would you go to church with me one time?" I said sure. So we made plans to go to the first Christian church in Indiana.

I haven't seen Gary in a long time, I wondered how he's been. Nick asked me who Gary was. I told him I worked with him at amusement park in St.Louis. I said he was a cool person. I also told Nick I wanted revenge on the guys that hurt my mother. At that time, the damage has been done. I told him I was a cult. Nick never judge me, but he didn't think I was the right choices in my life. I had a lot better friends now than the ones I was making in school or at work. It felt great to get a lot of bad stuff of my chest. I never felt that relieved in my life, but I was still acting out, I told Nick that I was seeing counseling. Nick told me he had a friend named Tommy. He was very quiet and didn't speak much. I was very wary of him at first till he told me he was also Christian. I thought he can also come over next time. For the first time, I felt like my life has changed. They didn't see that other side of me till later. One Saturday, he bought Tommy over. I asked Nick if he had a brother. He said yes, and his brother's name was Nathan or Nate. He didn't live with him. I remember saying I would like to meet him. Nick told me I will sooner or later you.

In early 2011, I wanted to get baptized. Me, Nick, and some friends were down playing basketball all day. It was so much fun and worked up a good sweat. I ran into guy name Jacob. We all decided to stop playing basketball and just listen to each other's stories. Jacob told us that he was in the army. We heard how he got God in his life. It was a very sad story, but it had a happy ending. When it was my turn, I told them parts of my story. It was a shock to everyone. I told them I was still struggling to get myself better and get the help. Jacob told me and Nick, "You're welcome to come to my house so we can go swimming and continue our chat. But then a few days later, I got to finally meet Nick's brother Nathan. He was such a nice guy. He was also a big teddy bear. We couldn't hang out too long that day because we both had things to do. Nick said, "I will bring Nate over, and we all can talk." I said that's fine with me.

Diana called me that night. We talked about my new friends and how good an influence they had on me. I told her I wish these were the people I met before all of my troubles began. At that point, I taught Nathan to watch horror movies. He wasn't a big horror movie fan like me and Nick. We all watched and ate pizza at my place. After the movie, Nathan didn't really care for the movie at all. He was Christian also. After we turned the television off, we all decide to go into the kitchen and we sat down to talk about our lives and God

I told Nate my story. I said I was still mad at God for what he was doing. It just seemed like no one could set me straight. I continued to head down the wrong path for myself and my friends. I didn't want to drag anyone down with me at all because I was still doing paranormal investigations till 2014. They didn't believe in ghost, they just think it was demons and not spirts. They had their own opinions, that's fine I was okay with that, but they weren't going to change me. I wasn't going to let them. Still I had mixed feelings about them. I didn't really know them too well. I only knew Nick for a couple of months, and I just met his brother. Now they were asking me if I would like to go to church with them. I said fine, but there were times I went, sometimes I had to make a story just not to go, and other times I didn't feel like getting out of bed.

On July 17, 2011, I got a call from Nick letting me know that Jacob wanted us to come to his house that day for a barbecue and swimming. I accepted. We all packed up and got ready to head to Jacob's house. Nick and Nate picked me up at my apartment complex. Jacob's house was a small but very beautiful place. He lived up the hill by the river so we would have to walk in the woods to get down to the river. It was awesome. I didn't swim in the river first time around, but they got into it so I just watch them. We still had a fun time. After we were done, we walked back up to his house through the woods. After we had dinner at Jacob's, we went out and made a big fire. We all sat around it and just talked about God. I told Jacob I wasn't ready to get baptized yet. I said, "Maybe next year, I will get baptized." It was just an excuse. Something was stopping me from getting it done. I always believed it could have been my past. I didn't want to let go of my past just yet. I didn't want to get baptized in front of a whole lot of people. I wasn't people person at that time. I had to overcome some of my fears. He just told me I need God's help to get me through my struggle. It felt like life was pretty much beating me down. I had to find a way to conquer it and start fresh.

It wasn't easy for me. I needed to read my Bible, which I wasn't. That was part of my problem. I didn't have anything to do with it at all. I told Jacob I have been through a lot in my life. I told him I was living a double life. I even told him about that Halloween night in 1989, that I wanted to beat down and hurt the two masked men for hurting my mom. He said, "Don't do that let. God handle them." Jacob explained to me that God wouldn't want me to take the law into my own hands. "Let God handle this. He's got this."

But I was so stubborn. I knew this was going to be a long journey ahead of me, but I wasn't going to give up the fight. No one else knew what my diagnosis was, not even the counselors I went to see. I told them that I might have PTSD with anxiety and depression. I don't know if the counselors diagnosed me correctly. I bet they thought I was crazy. At that time, I was around twenty-eight years old. I don't think they knew what they was doing actually. I told them what the symptoms were and that Paul had PTSD from the Vietnam War. Even though I wasn't in any kind of military, anyone can get PTSD.

There was one counselor I said some pretty ugly things to. She made me so mad. I wasn't going to let her win at all. She was threatening to call the police. I told her, "I want you to release me. I'm not going to see you anymore." She was actually pregnant then. Over time, I felt really bad about what I said to her and the baby. The next day, I told my friends about what I said. They had no idea what made me say something like that to her. I just flipped out on her. I thought she was bullying me and I had to stand my ground. I wasn't going to take it anymore from anyone. I never saw her again. I wanted to apologize to her for what I had said to her and her unborn baby. No one should be attacked like that. With everything that was actually happening at that time, I thought I was getting better. There were days when I was actually happy and other days when I wanted to take someone apart. It felt awful. It wasn't a pleasant feeling at all.

In late 2011, my real dad passed away. I went to the funeral and to the cemetery, but his stepson told me I wasn't welcome there, which made me very mad. I never got to meet him at all. I only saw pictures of him and his ashes.

8

Tragedies

The year 2012 passed me by. I still haven't got my life together, even though I was still working and I got ten credit hours in school to be a mortician. Although I was passing classes, also drawing classes, it was becoming very difficult for me to do my studies and there was a lot going on in my mind. After having a 4.0 GPA, it was getting very hard for me to concentrate. I figured I would get this done and take a break from it. I did get my thirteen credit hours in late 2012. I caught up with an old friend from amusement park. Gary and I reconnected. I invited him to church and introduced him to my friends. Nathan said after church that we should hang out. All was fine with that.

In early March of 2013, Diana called me and told me that my aunt was diagnosed with amyotrophic lateral sclerosis (ALS), also known as Lou Gehrig's disease. It was hard on Diana. I ask how Paul was. She said he's doing great. She told me that he wanted to take me to see a movie in July, *Dark Knight Rises*. Sounds great. But my brother and his wife had another child, another boy they named Aiden Wyatt. The nickname I give him was Wyatt Earp.

One day when I was on Facebook, one of the neighbors I used to hang out with passed away. That tore me up inside. He was one of the few who tried to get me back on my feet. On February 18, 2013, he died in the hospital. I went to the funeral and graveside service for him. He liked to collect toy cars as a hobby. Since he knew I wanted to be a funeral director, he gave me a toy car that was a hearse. I still have it to this day. It reminds of what I wanted to with my life. He left behind two kids and his wife. I still haven't gotten over his death. It was very sad because he died at a young age. He knew my real dad Jason. Just one month after my friend was gone, Diana called me from the nursing home to tell that Edna didn't have much time left. She couldn't walk or eat anymore. We used to visit them for family get-togethers. The year 2012 was the last time I saw her. Just a few weeks later, she passed away in March 2013. Diana was by her side, holding her hand as she passed peacefully.

In 2013, I finally got baptized. I also went to two funerals within a month apart. It was so devastated for me and the rest of our family. We were lost for words. No one can run from death. That's part of life. They year passed by quickly. Early 2014 on a warm sunny day in Union, Indiana, I got a call from Mom telling me that her twin sister was admitted into the Mercy hospital from chest pain. Well, that night and the next day, I was running a fever so I had my neighbor take me to Patient First. It turned out that I had strep throat, which was contagious. After I got home, I went straight to bed. The next day, I took my meds. I heard a strange noise coming from my ceiling. I could see part of the roof. I went over to tell one of my other neighbors. She came over to my place and told me she was going to get the landlord. When she came back, she said that she informed the maintenance man so he will be over as soon as he can. I told her I could hear something cracking and popping. The ceiling could come down at any minute. Then we heard the popping sound again. As soon I walked toward the screen door, I told her come toward me. Suddenly, the whole living room and part of the kitchen ceiling collapsed on top of her down. It also knock me out the front door. I had some lifesaving skills from being a part-time firefighter at one time. I ran outside to see what happened. Someone called 911 as I rushed back inside to get her out of the house. I had to dig through the pile of rubble to get her. We were afraid that more would come down so the police, fire trucks, and the ambulance rushed to the scene. My whole street was packed with emergency vehicles. They took her to the hospital. The landlord and the maintenance man

THE STRUGGLE WITHIN

came down. They heard what happened and rushed over to assess the damage. The fire department went into my apartment to see what caused the cave-in. When they first built that place, they didn't put in the right nails. They used screws to put up the dry walls. The police used yellow tape to keep everyone out of the house in case of another cave-in. I put some photos up on Facebook. My family saw the post and called me to ask me if I was okay. My brother had two sons, Ethan and Aiden, so I had to stay the night at my cousin's place. The next day, I walk back to my apartment to ask to my landlord if the fire chief been there to see it.

At that same time, I was going back and forth to the hospital and trying to get the apartment situation worked out. I wanted to get back in the apartment to get things I needed, but they wouldn't let me do that. At that point, I had to stay at the hotel close by so I could pack my things and move out. I didn't want to go back to live in that apartment complex. When they finally let me in a couple days later, I was so afraid of what could happen next. Maybe God was trying to tell me something and I wasn't listening to him at all. I visited my aunt at the hospital. She fell into a coma. We didn't know what else to dot. The whole family was up there, just waiting patiently in her room for a while. It has been a very long day. At some point, my cousin and I went to Pizza Hut for dinner. We were so exhausted that she took me back to the motel. I stay there till I found another apartment.

On that rainy Saturday afternoon, I got a called from Diana telling me that my aunt, her twin sister, didn't have much time left. That Monday, I found another apartment I could move into a couple of days later. I had to go back and forth to storage to get some of my stuff. My friends and my cousin helped me to get my stuff out from the storage company. Well, that very next day, toward the end of June on a beautiful Friday afternoon, my aunt passed away peacefully at 4:30 p.m. For the funeral, Douglas, my cousins, my uncle, and I were assigned to be pallbearers. The funeral was very hard and sad. That this had to happen in my family. I had to get away and visit friends I haven't seen them in a couple of months since the ceiling collapsed in my apartment.

Just a month after we buried my mom's twin sister, I got another phone calling saying that Paul wasn't doing good. I stopped working at the YMCA in 2013 after having three hernia surgeries so I just stayed home. I wanted to go back to school but everything that happened kept me away from going back. In August 2014, Diana called me to say that Paul was fading fast. She and friend Jackie were in the room with him. He couldn't talk anymore. He was raising his hands in the air as if asking God to take him home. Mom told me that nine months before he died, he was saved. Paul's mom arrived on September 14, 2014. She stayed there till 11:00 p.m. to be with her son. At around 2:30 a.m., Diana called me to tell me Paul passed away. I never went to see him because I didn't want to see him in bad shape. I couldn't come to terms with his death. He went to his grave never knowing who hurt my mom that night. Thursday, September 18 was the day of the funeral. He was buried at Jefferson Barracks in Indiana. Mom told me he was drinking so much because he was in pain from lung cancer. We never knew he had cancer. That broke my heart with what I did to him. If I knew that he had lung cancer, I would have never gotten into arguments with him. If the police caught the men who hurt his wife, he would have been really happy in his grave. It hasn't been the same without him. He stopped drinking about a year before he passed away. The cycle of going from funeral to funeral didn't seem like it would end anytime soon. It was hard on all of us. I told my mom and grandma I was so ready for this year to end. I tried to find some comfort about everything that took place that year. It felt like a nightmare.

I always called my mom to check in on her. I had my brother Douglas move next to her so he could help her out and take her to the grocery shopping. So my brother moved his two kids and wife to where we grew up. I thought back to the relationship me and Paul had, even though he wasn't my real dad. I remember him taking me to see the *Dark Knight Rises*. He was trying to make up for the lost time. To this day, I still feel very bad for the way I treated him. I thought about it a lot. He was there when Jason wasn't around. He was the one who changed my dirty diapers. I felt like I let him down when I couldn't be a funeral director. It would kill me to be a funeral director and just see those sad families.

Just before my brother's birthday, another one our uncles passed away on Paul's side of the family. It was a rough year. Just a month before Thanksgiving and Christmas, it was going to be even rough for us to know that Paul wasn't going to be around for both holidays. Our family had to try and deal with it the best way we could to get through the holidays. My fear of death was hitting me so hard. The only good thing was that 2014 was finally over. However, we soon had to deal with another tragic death in early march. My mom called to tell me that her mom wasn't acting right so she contacted our uncle to go check on her mom. My uncle didn't think she was acting right too so he took her to the hospital. They had her admitted after she had two major strokes. There was too much pressure and bleeding in her brain. When we arrived at the hospital, she was awake and alert but could barely talk. Her left arm and leg were paralyzed. She just looked at us all. It was just going to get rough from here on out. I asked God, "Please help us! We were all hurting because we just lost two family members. She was grieving over her daughter." We couldn't take any more funerals. One aunt that drove from Arkansas, and one cousin drove from Panama City Beach, Florida. It was just completely chaotic that day when everyone got to the hospital. The whole family waited in the waiting room till the doctors could came to tell us what their plan was. When the doctors came in, they asked permission to send her to a different hospital to open her brain to take pressure off. We asked t would she be like afterward. They said more likely she would be a vegetable. My uncle said we will take a vote because he had no idea what to do. He went around the room to ask us all. I said we shouldn't let her suffer more than she already was.

I still ask myself to this day if I gave the right answer to my uncle. I hope God would forgive me for what I did then I felt like that her life was in everybody's hands, including mind. I don't know if I did the right thing. My cousin and I stayed the night at mom's house after dropping by Walmart. My cousin cooked lasagna. It was a great dinner, but we were all worried. We just had a weird feeling that night. Me and my cousin got into her car and rushed back to the hospital to check if she was okay. We peeked into her room, and the nurse said she was okay. That made us feel a lot better. The next day, my cousin went home. She told me to call her if anything happened. I assured her I would. My friend and I stayed at the hospital between seven to eight days. I had to go home to shower, but I slept in the waiting room all that time. I went home eventually till we got another phone saying, "She could go tonight."

So after spending eight nights at the hospital, I thought, How can that be? That's so weird!" I had a neighbor drive me up to the hospital. The doctors and my uncle talked about moving her to the nursing home where my one aunt work at. The next day, the ambulance transported her to the nursing home. My mom stayed with her. I was at home cooking dinner when the phone rang, It was my mom telling me that my grandma's breathing was starting to slow down little by little. I knew right then that she wasn't going to live to much longer. We just had to make the best of it. I prayed to God not to let her suffer anymore. At 4:15 p.m., she passed away peacefully in her sleep. I thanked God thanks for ending her suffering. It might sound mean, but we all didn't want her suffering any longer. I called my cousin via Facebook to let her know. My uncle called the rest of the family to inform them of her death and when the arrangements would be. The next day, my cousin drove up all the way from Panama City Beach. I had to call my landlord to let her stay till the funeral was over. The day before the visitation, we drove to Diana's house. She told us she wrote a speech for the funeral and was nervous about. I offered do it. I did it once at Paul's funeral. It was going to be nerve-racking, but I know I had the strength to do it.

We went to visit him before we leave for the funeral home. For the funeral, I wore black dress pants with blue shirt and tie and a blue vest. My cousin was also in black dress pants and blue shirt. When we got to Midlawn Funeral Home, we sat outside in our cars till the doors opened. Then we walked into the chapel and saw her lying there. She was so beautiful. The did a great job on her. But once the visitation was over, my uncle threw himself over the casket, talking to his mom and weeping. It was very emotional. After half an hour, he finally calmed down and told us we all have a big day tomorrow so we need our sleep. My cousin and I went back to my apartment. We decided to stay the night at Diana's house where I grew up. I had a hard time sleeping because I knew that I had to get up next day and speak in front of a bunch of people. I just had to think real hard that night what I was going to say and how I was going to say it. I slept in Paul and Mom's room. I was so stressed out, I ended up losing a lot of hair over the years. After hardly getting any sleep, I got up and got ready. It was going to be very be very difficult for us, just a year after burying Paul and my aunt.

After the pastor spoke, it was time for my speech. Nervous, I got up, took a deep breath, and delivered the eulogy for a few minutes. I ended with the poem then I said, "We will never forget. You will always be in our memories forever." It was the same speech I gave in Paul's funeral. At the graveside service, the family sat down in the chairs while the rest were standing up. After it was done, we all went to my uncle's house for dinner. Diana, my cousin, and I went back to the cemetery to look at her grave. The dirt was caving a little so we had to give our uncle a call. He then called the funeral home to fix. I went back a couple of weeks later, and they did fix it Just a couple of months after we said good-bye to our grandma, my sister-in-law was once again pregnant. We were all hoping for a little girl this time then she was done having kids.

For the rest of 2015, we tried to move on from all the deaths, think about the happy times, and try to enjoy life. But 2016 had its ups and downs for me. My dreams were getting worse and my temper had gotten out of hand with everything that's been happening to me and my family. But in May 16th of that year, my neighbor wanted me get some window blinds for my windows. He was high as a kite so he wanted me to drive. I only had my permit so I couldn't be driving the car unless they had their license and insurance on the car. He wanted me to drive though I told him I didn't feel confident to drive. I haven't had much time to practice so I didn't want to take that chance. He just kept begging me and begging till I finally broke down and said yes. So I got in the driver's side and buckled in. He did too. When I started the car, I was beginning to have a panic attack. As I was pulling out, trying to turn, I hit the wrong paddle and shot down the hill. The car knock out the fence and gate, tore up the yard, and did damage to the garage. Someone called 911. By the time they got there, we were already out of the car, all shook up. I went between two trees and miraculously wasn't killed or hurt anyone else. It was very scary. I didn't know what to do. My neighbor got put in handcuffs. When the police took my report, I told them honestly that I was trying to hit the break but I got confused with the paddles. A couple of weeks later, I got a letter saying I have to pay for the damages amounting to $4,100. I didn't have that kind of money so I had to find me a lawyer. Thankfully, I knew her mom and my uncle went to school together and were pretty close. She induce me to her daughter, Rachel. Any paperwork that I got I had to take straight to Rachel. In August of that year, my niece was born. My brother and sister-in-law named her Raelynn.

9

Wedding

It was February 21, 2017, a Saturday. I got a call from Nathan asking me if he could come over to speak to me about something. I asked him if I did anything wrong. He said no. At that point, I was pretty paranoid. I had been like that ever since my mom got attacked. I didn't trust anyone so I had to keep my guard up this time. I was also doing counseling. Nathan came over to ask me if I would attend the wedding if he married Anna. At first I said no because I really didn't feel all too comfortable hanging around with a bunch of people I didn't know. He kept pleading until I said, "Okay, that's fine." He said I was one of his best friends. I didn't want to let him down.

One day at my counselor's appointment, I told her I was very excited to attend the wedding. We talked about that Halloween night and my real dad. I wasn't really interested in being a funeral director anymore after Paul passed away and finding out that I had depression, PTSD, anxiety disorder, and panic attacks. I was so relieved about admit it. I was a bit scared because I didn't know how to tell the people around me that I had all these issues. I didn't know what their response was going to be. I felt such relief that I was getting meds to take care of my problems. When I got depressed, I would lock myself up in the house. I though the only thing that helped me during those times was watching horror movies. It was eating me up inside that I had a mental illness with everything that happened in my life. I wish I could be a normal young man. It wasn't easy for me to live a happy life. I knew what was causing a lot of the nightmares, dreams, and flashbacks. I felt like some of the darkness left me that day, but I still have dark thoughts in my mind that I keep fighting by going to church, reading my Bible, and talking to my friends. The horror movies weren't helping me either. I saw a psychiatrist about my scary dark thoughts. I didn't know that it was part of my PTSD. I tried to keep my mind off it by walking around and listening to music. I had a lot of trauma in my life, which was why I talked to them about something positive, like the wedding. I also tried to get rid of all the negative people in my life. I always give people a second chance, but if I kept hanging out with them, they would get me in trouble. I had to ditch them.

One night, I had awful nightmare. I dreamt I was in hell. People were screaming for mercy. They couldn't leave the dark pit because there were locked in. It felt like I was really there, but then I tried to wake up. Before I could, I saw the devil face-to-face. He had an evil grin, laughing maniacally at me. I woke up yelling, drenched in sweat. In my dream, he wouldn't stop laughing. It felt real, I could practically smell burnt flesh. I went to see my counselor the next day. I told her what the devil was doing and what I saw in my dream. She told me I was fighting a war between good and evil and I could be fighting for a long time. I had to stop watching horror movies I think parts of it was affecting me, but I also thought it had something to do with the cult. I was already at war with my religion. My counselor said I needed to talk with a pastor, priest, or both. When I did woke up I also was repeating that I will beat you and you will be beaten by God. I had to keep this between me and counselor.

At that point in my life, I couldn't put my guard down anymore I had to keep fighting and fighting. I am still fighting Satan to this day. After my fourth surgery, my body was getting tired and I was getting very frustrated. I believed I was getting tested by God. I knew he wouldn't put me through anything that I couldn't handle. I knew God would always have my back and wouldn't let anything happen to me at all.

Right before summer started, we all went swimming at the river on a nice warm day. Nick, Nathan, Anna, Tommy, and I had a great day swimming and barbecuing. Every summer, we would usually go swimming. One time, my buddy drove to Target because he was obsessed with an actress. Someone who worked at Target looked like that actress. We were very upset about the situation, however, we all supported him. I even went to his court hearing for his sentencing. In the next few weeks, we had to plan for a wedding. Gary was still working at amusement park while Nick was working at a factory in Union, Indiana. Nathan and I went apartment hunting for him and soon-to-be wife then we went to pick out a ring. After we picked out the rings, me and Nathan went out to eat at Sonic. We got a lot of things accomplished that day. Anna and Nate met at a church event one year ago. We were all so happy that they were planning to get married.

I was waking up finally release that this was a family thing we would do everything together. That's how a family was we were one big group of friends even at times we would swim at Ashley parents' house when she would come up from Kansas City. My mind would be of I wouldn't worry about anything only except my stomach was starting to act up again. I was puking every five minutes. At first I thought I had the flu bug or stomach bug. I wanted to see my doctor to see if they can find out what was wrong with me, but when I called him, he was booked up. He couldn't get me in till December. I felt like I was dying because my illness was getting worse and worse. I didn't know what to do. Nathan already paid for my tuxedo. I talked to him and his fiancée about my health situation. He just told me to try to make the best of it. I said, "Okay, I will try to do my best."

We had one last court for Nathan to see what his punishment will be. When the Judge came in, we forgot to stand up. Boy oh boy did we hear from the sheriff deputy that day. He told us that the next time we don't stand up, we will be in big trouble. We look at each other and discussed if we heard the deputy say "Rise." After a recess break, we made sure stand up the next time the judge came into the courtroom. The ankle monitor was taken off a while back. He got two years of probation and was ordered to report to his probation officer every two to three weeks. In summer that year, he got baptized. Gary and I helped out, which was a privilege and an honor.

As we was getting close to Halloween and Thanksgiving before the wedding, we all spent the fall painting pumpkins. One thing was still on my mind, that faithful Halloween night. Every year, I would celebrate that time by looking for the two masked men. I was doing my best to track them down no matter what. I had to focus on my health and the wedding.

On a cold brisk October evening, we all went out and played some football in the yard even though I was sick and spent most of the time I would be in the bathroom. I told everyone I couldn't wait to see the doctor about this problem. That following Tuesday, I went for a upper GI on my stomach. I didn't get the test results back till a couple days later It turned out I would need another surgery because the mesh came apart. It was making me sick. I couldn't eat or I would just puke. The doctor was the one who actually called about my results. They moved my appointment until after the wedding. That's great news.

We all sat around and talk about the wedding stuff. Nathan made me and his brother as the groomsmen, but we had to find one more person to be a groomsman since we only had two guys and three bridesmaids. I suggested Gary. I was sure he wouldn't mind. So I called Gary up and told him that Nathan wanted to speak with him. He said he will be come over in a few months. I went back into the living room and told him Nathan Gary will be over. About five minutes later, Gary showed up. Nathan and Nick sat him down. "We got something we wanted to ask you. Gary, would you like to be our third groomsman?" Gary said yes right away. He would have to go get fitted for a tuxedo. Nathan and Anna had to discuss some wedding songs with us, like "Can't Help Falling in Love" sung by Elvis Presley and a song by America, a seventies rock group called "Todays the Day." We all thought those songs would work. At that time, Ashley was home in Kansas City to visit her parents and friends. After dinner, we played some board games. It was the best night ever. This was the first wedding for me and Nick. I called my mom to tell her the good news that I was going to be in the here in a few months. She was so excited to see me happy. However, I still had to deal with the stomach issues.

THE STRUGGLE WITHIN

Just a month in a half till the wedding, we had to get ready for Thanksgiving and a hunting trip. I was so excited for two things. I actually went to Sullivan, Indiana, and spent two nights there with Frank. The next morning, we both got up and headed out into the woods. It was so peaceful out there, that's where I wanted to be. It was time for me to hunt l a deer for myself. I had seen a lot, just never kill one before. It was my fifth year trying to get a good one. Either way, it was a fun time to be away from everything. Once I got back to Union, Indiana, I was glad to be back home. I didn't have to be worried about my struggles or anything. Just a few days after being home, Thanksgiving was coming up in two weeks. I went grocery shopping to get everything ready for the big feast. After Thanksgiving, Anna would have her bachelorette party. On December 9, we would have our bachelor party for Nathan.

After I had Thanksgiving dinner by myself, Gary picked me up. We went to Black Thursday Christmas shopping. It was a lot of fun to do at night, like it was watching football. The next day, I decided to stay home and just catch up on sleep well. On December 1, 2017, just a couple of weeks away from the wedding, I couldn't wait to see the doctor. I was more ready for the doctor than the wedding. I actually put money for the bachelor party. After to dinner so that day of the 9th I didn't have to cook anything. I was actually pretty happy that day. I asked Nathan once if we could stay the night at his apartment a day before the wedding. He said sure. I went to get my new glasses for the wedding. I love them. I had to wear them to the bachelor's party. Nathan and Nick's dad drove us. We were all very excited. I wish Paul was around. He would have been so proud of me doing this wedding. Paul would have been proud of anything I've done. I had a lot of memories to look back on all of these years. I miss dad so much. For some reason, Halloween 1989 popped back up in my mind. It was very uncomfortable to think about something when I am about to do something very fun.

I was still fighting the mesh issue. I was hoping to get through one night without any problems. The first place we stopped at for our bachelor's party was Golden Corral. They some great food. We even made some jokes about our groom, and the lady who worked there kept teasing him. It was a fun night. After dinner, my stomach was feeling great. I hoped I didn't puke. We all went to the mall and split up. Nick and I went to the JCPenny inside the mall. We bought some stuff there then we all went to another mall where we got our pitchers. Talking with the big himself Santa Claus now I didn't want to get into the group photo at all I was just feeling that great the groom was sitting right in front of Santa while we was all behind him that was the funniest moment ever. We got back very late in the morning so I didn't go to church. Actually, no one did either. I stayed home to slept and watch football because I was puking once again. On Sunday the 10th, I watched the Baltimore Ravens play that day. They beat the Los Angeles Rams.

The following week, we were getting nervous for the big day. Friday was the rehearsals for the wedding so I just stayed home and rested that week. I didn't really do anything at all. When Friday came around, we went up to city hall for the wedding reception. Then we all went to Nathan's house. Anna went with her family. That night, we was all very nervous and excited. The only one who wasn't there yet was Ashley. She was driving up here during the rehearsals. We wanted to get it right the first time but had to go over it twice. Then we went to city hall for the rehearsal dinner for a lot of great food. I was hoping not to get sick or let anyone see me get sick. After dinner, Nick and his roommate Tommy went back to their place. Gary and I stayed the night at Nathan and Anna's new apartment. Gary slept in the same bed with Nathan while I slept on the couch. We needed our sleep for the big day. I didn't get sick that night but had a rough night of sleep because I was nervous about the wedding. I also had insomnia, which had been very hard on me and my body.

On the big day, I got up at about nine o'clock, took a shower, went to Fricks to get something very light to eat, and then I got dressed in my tuxedo. At about two o'clock, we headed for the church to get ready. When we got to First Christian Church, we all had to stay upstairs while the women were downstairs. The wedding started at 3:30 p.m. in the afternoon. We got our pitchers toking and we got our flowers on our jackets and they us they were ready for us. Nathan had to wait in the chapel. We were walking toward the front but stopped to get our pictures taken. By that time we got into the chapel, the bride walked. Anna looked stunningly beautiful. It was a great wedding. I actually had tears in my eyes a few times. We got all choked up. After the wedding, we all stood in line and shook everyone's hand. That was nerve-racking for me.

Once all the guest headed to city hall, we had to get our pictures taken with the bride and groom. The first I sat down, my stomach was hurting me. I was like, *Oh no! Here we go again.* It hurt so bad, I had to run to the bathroom but nothing came out. We were waiting for the party bus to get to the church. At city hall, I felt more sick than ever before. When our name was announced by the nice gentleman, we took our seats in the front of everybody. I had to run and get me some Sprite and 7 Up. I tried to eat some food. That didn't work either so now our friend Ashley had to run to the store to get me something. Nathan was nervous. The medicine didn't work on me. I was in the bathroom for the rest of the reception. I felt really bad so my friends took me home. I went to bed and didn't get up till the next morning. I didn't go to church at all because I was exhausted. I turned the television on to some football and slept through it. I wanted to run to the store to pick up some Sprite and 7 Up. I was still vomiting till about four in the afternoon. When I finally felt better, Gary came to pick up the tuxedo. He bought me a 7 Up.

On Tuesday, I went to the doctor's office. They told me I would need another surgery, making it my fifth one in a year's time. It was getting old. So I didn't have surgery till after all the holidays. I spent Christmas in the bathroom, puking every five minutes, but I did make it through the holidays without having sharp pains. On January 15, 2018, I finally had my surgery. I was hoping this will finally do the trick. After six weeks of restrictions, I was able to do anything again. I felt pretty good as time went on. I was so ready for it to be done one day. I was watching *Silver Bullet* on Blu-ray. I just stayed in my house with the doors and the curtains shut. I was starting to have one of my moods. I didn't want to do anything. I had moments when I don't want to talk or hang out with anyone. I just wanted to be by left alone.

It's been four years since Paul passed. Paul's mom often called, and we'd talk about Paul. She would be crying over the phone. She too had poor health. We didn't think she would make it from the pain of losing all three of her boys. She grieve over all three of them. She was one of my favorite grandmas. It hasn't been the same since he's gone. There were times when me and my mom didn't get alone. It was so hard for us both. She wasn't even over her husband death. It hit her really hard because she had to watch four of her family members die right in front of her. The only way I got through Paul's death was to watch horror movies and *The Walking Dead*. I bawled that day when we had to carry his casket to his final resting place. I almost forgot what he sounds like. Every holiday was different since he wasn't around to meet his third grandchild. Paul was wounded in the Vietnam War, shot in the shoulder, and also suffered from PTSD. He was drinking so much because he had cancer and never mention it to us. It was a lesson that life is way too short. We have to live our life one day at a time. You never know when your time might be up. Spend time with the ones you love. Do whatever it takes to live and to make it out there in the world.

10

Life

On May 20, 2018, I got a phone call from my mom telling me that put Paul's mom in a nursing home. She was going blind in both of her eyes. She wanted to stay and live in her apartment but her sister and other family member had no choice. She didn't like that, but it was for the best. As for me, I had some more health issues. My elbow was killing me. The doctors end up sending me to a specialist who told me I had tennis elbow. We go through struggles every day in life. We have to live the best way we could to make it in the world.

My friends and I went to Nate and Anna's house for a barbecue. We had fun playing frisbee and football in the yard. There were times we would all go to the local high school football field to play some touch football in the rain or snow. We felt like the NFL. We had great time. The summer was almost over.

Diana kept in touch with me about Paul's mom. We just lost four family members on Diana's side. It was very hard to lose my grandma. Our family been through tough times, but we had learn to fight through them and move on. We were still grieving for the people that we lost. I didn't even go near funeral homes or graveyards for a while. I was still mad over losing my stepdad. It wasn't easy for me after suffering a lot in life, from my real dad to the 1989 Halloween incident, but I made the best of it. I never showed my sadness in front of people.

By the time 2019 arrive, I need one more surgery. This time, it was a little bit longer than the previous five surgeries. The doctors had to reopen me up and take out the old mesh and scrape the old scar tissue. On top of everything, they found three more small hernias. They fixed it up so I wouldn't need a another surgery again. This last surgery woke me up. I realized that I was mean and hateful to people in my life. I had to really focus to get it fix once and for all. God could take me home at any time so I wouldn't been able to apologize to anyone I was mean to.

After my surgery, I woke up in the recovery room. I didn't know what was going on except that the doctors were moving me from one bed to another. I put up a fight. Once they moved me back to the original bed, I felt the bed moving as I fell asleep. They moved me up to the sixth floor. I remember needing to use the bathroom. I was in so much pain, I had a hard time getting up out of bed. I tried so hard to force myself to get up. I didn't want to stay in the hospital like the last time. I argued with the nurses. They knew I wanted to go home and understood I was very crabby. I did apologize to the nurses for acting like a fool. What hurt me was getting as shot in my stomach now that hurt I wasn't use to having a needle in my stomach but I actually felt pretty good. I asked the nurse to please turn up the air-conditioning in my room because I was burning up. They put a fan in my room. That night, I didn't have much sleep. I had to sleep in a chair right next to the fan for the rest of my stay in the hospital. It was winter so it was cold outside. I was used to the cold because. I always kept my fan and air conditioner on through the winter. When I finally came home that next day, I didn't really eat anything because I was too sore. I did get up and walk around like my doctor told me to. I was hoping this would be my very last surgery. This surgery made me think that life was too short to be mad at the world. While I was working on getting better, I thought about all those years I wasted being angry and worried about the two men who hurt Diana. I had to figure a way to overcome this fear and move on with my life. I needed to start fresh. At that time, I was gaining weight from eating way too much.

When February came, I went back to amusement park to become an entertainer. I had to try on some costumes for a character. I needed to stop drinking soda, which I had been drinking for thirty-six years. Just working in the summertime in character might help me sweat off the weight. Right after surgery, I did lose some weight. I think I was just eating to take the pain away from me. After I tried the costumes on, they told me they will call me back in a few weeks. Well, a few weeks went by and I never heard from them. Even when I called, I still haven't heard from them. When they finally called, they told me, "It wasn't you, but it was something to do with the costume." The interview went great. That's why I went out and tried the costumes on to see if they fit me. I still couldn't do much because I was on restrictions from the doctor. Once I was off, I went back out there for another job interview. I was going to try out as a lifeguard. I couldn't do that because they didn't want me to wear sleeves. Because I had big tattoos, I had to wear sleeves. So I said, "Okay, train me on rides then."

I got rehired after I was unjustly blamed for something that wasn't my fault back in 2004. I was still pretty upset with them about but that went away fast since I got my job back. I had to do training on the ride because I haven't work on rides since 2004. Finally something great was happening for me again. I was going back to a place where I first work back in 1999. I was so grateful that God was watching over me when I worked on the rides. I would pray about it. That very next weekend, I was out there on job training when I felt very nervous and scared about the whole thing. I had no idea what I might get myself into. I was going to be very patient about it and just relax. However, when I finally was done with training, the nervousness and my fears came back. I had a hard time trusting anyone there because of some of the crew. I felt very nervous about the whole thing so I just tried to mind my own business and just do my job. I was on my main ride one day when things took a turn for the worse. On my first day back, I get yelled at by one of my coworkers. She wasn't a lead or a supervisor. I didn't know if she was having a bad day or what. We started to get into a heated discussion. I was so confused about the ride. I haven't done it in so long so on my lunch break I asked to be taken off from rides and switch over to the grounds. My anxiety was kicking in. I was unusually very uncomfortable on rides. I had some flashbacks of that day I came on for my shift and the ride broke down, which was so weird. I was very uncomfortable being on the ride. I just worked grounds till Fright Fest tryouts in July. I only work one day on grounds after training then I quit my job. I think God was telling me I didn't belong there anymore.

I am so happy that my nephews and niece weren't born yet when I was bitter about life at the time. I didn't want them to see their uncle like that. When Paul passed away, it took a lot of me. I didn't know what to do anymore. No one in my family did. It was just a crushing moment. He would've wanted us to move on in and be happy. He didn't want us to worry about him. I always told my friends or someone who lost a family member or a friend that God has a special place for their loved ones in heaven. Looking back, I just sat there and wasted time away. I wanted Paul to be happy. I know he's looking down at me and saying, "That's my stepson."

So I been doing a lot of thinking. Maybe someday in time I will go back and finish mortuary school. I was so unsure before, but now I was determined to go back one day to do what I love doing. I wanted to help other people deal with the loss of a love one and tell them my story about how to deal with life and death. We all have to get through life by believing in God. Faith is something very important to me know, even though I am still having my ups and downs once in a while. I know God is helping me get through those rough times. The most important part of my life is God. I have gotten a lot better with my anger issues. It taught me to love again, but at the same time, I have to keep my guards up and not let the devil beat me as I sit back and watch the world destroy itself. There's still good people out there who can make this world a better place, not the way it is now. Me holding grudges toward people is not going to make this world a better place.

Mental illness is a worst thing to have in life. Having PTSD, anxiety, depression, and panic attacks makes it rough for me, but I have to learn to get through it and be strong for everyone around me. On August 16, 2019, I was getting angrier. Dark thoughts were running through my mind again. I finally told the devil, "I will beat you at your own game. If you want to attack me, I will attack back. You will not beat me like you have done in the past." My past still haunts me to this day a lot. PTSD is very scary, but I know that I will defeat this once and for all with the help of my my psychiatrist, God, my family, and my friends. They got me this far. I have come so far, I won't stop now. I might have to deal with it, but I will overcome my fear of Halloween. I have to confront the fear that bought me down to my knees. After going to jail three times, I would never go back to that place ever again. It's not a place where anyone should be. It all came down to me having made some very bad choices. I wasn't a good role model for anyone at that time. Now I can tell my kids one day, "Don't ever make choices that's going to get you into trouble with the law or maybe even lose your life." I do apologize for everything I have done to everyone. Everyday life is a struggle, but I am pushing and pushing. I know I can make a difference in someone's life. It's not good to have an ego, it's not worth it. You have to make the right choices in life.

As I continued to go to church, my dark side started to fade away little by little each day. I would like to help homeless veterans get a nice place to sleep where they are not exposed to freezing or hot weather. It's hard to see that happen to veterans who fought for our freedom. I was working on becoming a musician. I believe God had other plans for me. So I stopped playing drums and guitar and just be myself as a person. I wondered what my life would be like for people trying to be someone they're really not. My psychiatrist tells me to imagine what seven-year-old me would do. I tell you what I would do. I would hug and hold on to that seven-year-old me and tell him that everything will be okay and it would work itself out. God wants me to explore what I want to be in my life.

In early September, I saw that darkness can be defeated by the light. It got me through rough times. My counselor told me to confront the holiday that I was more afraid of. I been testing myself to get through Halloween. I know that the world is a dangerous place. There's only a few people I can trust and I have hard time making new friends, but I try not to let it affect my everyday life. I have been dealing with the PTSD and panic attacks for a long time. I struggled lot to beat the demons that lead me into this horrible situation. There were times I was so scared of going out for a walk. I always had to make sure that no one was behind me. That's how paranoid I was. I got scared for my mom every Halloween. I had to make sure that she doesn't pass out candy alone because Paul was no longer around. There's been times I would not even come out of my home because of the depression, but I am starting to confront my fears once and for all. I know times has been very difficult for me, but I have gotten through life with God by my side. I have been feeling safer during Halloween night so I finally went to Fright Fest at amusement park in St. Louis. It was a very fun event I stood up to my fears and face them head on, but I still have problems with it once in a while. I let my guard down in the past, now I am standing tall to take back what was mine and not let the devil get in the way of my life, even though he sometimes threw curveballs.

You don't have to be in the military to have PTSD, anyone witnessed a traumatic event can get it. I believe that good can will take down evil. I wish I could have a different outcome. I would never want to live the nightmare that I have live through for thirty-seven years of my life, but I have shown plenty of times that anyone can conquer life and beat demons. You would just need the proper care, treatment, and good solution that would help you overcome darkness. For you to have a good life is to not put your guard down against anyone who thinks you are weak. Lot of people did. That's why I got beat up by words and had to fight to keep living. I am very ashamed at not doing anything about it when the problem first occurred. Since then I have learned from my mistakes and not to let people talk me into doing things, I am not comfortable with. However, I still struggle with a lot of things. I don't have the nightmares or flashbacks like I used to, only once and a while. Sometimes it affects me and the people around me. Sometimes my mood is happy and other days not so much, but I always find a way to beat it and not let the devil get inside of my head. There are times I need to move on with life and tell myself that I will never find the two men so I might as well live a normal life. I have been searching for thirty-seven years. The more I am doing that, the more I missing out in bigger things. God wouldn't want me to keep torturing myself. I just need to go out, smile more, be myself, and not let the little things get to me anymore. It's been a roller coaster for me, but I am learning not to let it bug me or get it stuck in my head.

It has been five years since my dad died. When I think of him, I always remember him taking us to the movies. *Ghostbusters 2* was the one movie we saw back in 1989. We used to sit around the table to talk about the movies. I think that's what got me into the paranormal stuff as an adult. Unfortunately, my mom is still affected by what happened that Halloween night. We usually talk on the phone once in a while.

11

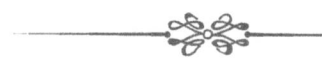

Diagnosed

Ever since I went back to counseling in 2017, I understood why I was acting out. I needed to be a better person. I have to live with this forever, but I don't have to be worried of it bringing me down. That's not going to bring me down on my knees. I will keep on walking and living everyday life like a normal person and just be happy. The panic attacks, depression, and anxiety will show its face from time to time. I continue to get help for it. When I was first diagnosed, I was so scared. I had nowhere to run. I always pray that God will show me how to deal with us, and he really help a lot. It's like I have been reborn. Sometimes it gets the best of me. Even though I have insomnia, I don't let it get me down. I will find a way to fight through it.

PTSD is very common. A lot of people has it. Even my mom has it, but she blocks it out of her mind and try to not let it get to her. The only way I can keep it off my mind is to keep busy and stay active. I don't even let the bullying get to me as bad anymore. Sometimes I have to stand up for myself and not let it affect me like it used to. My condition stopped me plenty of times in finding a woman in my life because I would always get mad at them even though they're not even doing anything wrong. I have always been very impatient with people, but I am working hard on being patient. I don't want to put any woman I'm with in a spot that would make her feel uncomfortable. The mental illness makes it was so hard for me to tell if people were comfortable with me or not. When I finally had the courage to tell my friends and family, it actually got easy for me.

However there's been people out there that your get over it or your fine the problem is you can get over it with the help. But the problem with that is no one will ever know what you went through unless they went through it themselves. Yes, it can happen to other people all over the world. You have to learn to live with it and move on, which I tried many times. It felt like I have been let down. I let it get to me. If I wasn't getting the help I needed, it could be worse. Talking to someone will help you. It worked for me. I was beginning to feel more like myself, as normal as I can be. Not many people come to terms with their problems. If you really think you need to be happy in life to get through it and you're not happy with yourself, how can you make anyone else happy? Be yourself. Don't pretend to be someone else that you're really not. Don't ever let anyone tell you no different that you can't make something out of life the best way to show them that you can is to do it. Show them that you can do whatever you want. Life may not be easy, but make the best of it as much you can.

That's what my parents always told me to do in life. I learned to figure out a way to help other people who might be in rough spot. You never know what that person is going through or what they're thinking. That person might be in trouble or just hurting. Listen to them and try to help them as much you can. You never know when they might need that extra hand. I learned never look down on someone who might be homeless or have a disability. They are a human being just like. Try to show them love with kindness and stand by their side. Everyone needs a hand once in a while. As I continue to walk the straight and narrow and improve my life, I want to be a better role model to my niece, my two nephews, and anyone around me. I am looking forward to sharing my story with people I have never met or even talked to. My friends, family, and God have given me the best opportunity to help others. Once I finally beat these illnesses, I can finally live a more peaceful life. I will never let anyone stand in the way of that. Just remember, you have only once chance to make something out of your life.

> *The Lord is my shepherd; I shall not want. He maketh to lie down in green pastures: he leadeth me beside the still waters. He restoreth my soul: he leadeth me in the paths of righteousness for his name's sake. Yea, though I walk through the valley of the shadow of death, I will fear no evil: for thou art with me; thy rod and thy staff they comfort me. Thou preparest a table before me in the presence of mine enemies: thou anointest my head with oil; my cup runneth over. Surely goodness and mercy shall follow me all the days of my life: and I will dwell in the house of the Lord forever.*
>
> —Psalm 23 (KJV)

About the Author

My name is Daniel Burks. I am an author who struggled to face my personal demons. After having fought my own demons for year, I found the light of redemption. While I am still fighting my anxiety, PTSD, depression, and panic attacks, I also fight the horrible nightmares from the tragic Halloween night of 1989 when my real dad told my mom not to bring me back ever again, which left me with questions and answers.

CPSIA information can be obtained
at www.ICGtesting.com
Printed in the USA
LVHW041213020820
662185LV00003B/956